Michael Kwamena
John Tosh
Richard Waller
Michael Tidy

African History in Maps

Longman

Longman Group UK Limited
Longman House, Burnt Mill, Harlow,
Essex CM20 2JE, England
and Associated Companies throughout the world.

First published 1982
Ninth impression 1992

Set in 10/12 Plantin

Printed in Hong Kong
WC/09

British Library Cataloguing in Publication Data
   African history in maps.
      I. Africa — Historical geography — Maps
      I. Kwamena — Poh, Michael
      9II'.6   G2446.SI

      ISBN 0-582-60331-5

Library of Congress Cataloging in Publication Data
Main entry under title:

African history in maps:
   Includes index.
   I. Africa — Historical geography.
   I. Kwamena — Poh, M.   II. Longman Group Ltd.
III. Title.
G2446.SIA4 1981 9II'.6   81-675343
ISBN 0-582-60331-5   AACR2

The cover picture is reproduced by courtesy of the
Trustees of the British Museum.

ISBN 0-582-60331-5

Contents

Map

1 Physical Geography *1*

2 Peoples of Africa *2*

3 North-West Africa and North-East Africa (Egypt and the Nile Valley and Ethiopia), 11th to 14th centuries *4*

4 North-West Africa, 16th to 18th centuries *6*

5 North-East Africa (Egypt and the Nile Valley and Ethiopia), 16th to 18th centuries *8*

6 West Africa to about 1600 *10*

7 First European contacts with West Africa, c. 1450 to c. 1800 *12*

8 West African states, 1600 to 1800 *14*

9 The Atlantic slave trade to 1808 *16*

10 Empires and kingdoms in Central and Eastern Africa, c. 1400 to c. 1800 *18*

11 The East African coast and the Indian Ocean, 700 to 1500 *20*

12 The European powers in the Indian Ocean and the Portuguese penetration of Africa, 1500 to 1800 *22*

13 The East African coast and Madagascar, 1500 to 1840 *24*

14 Southern Africa, 1652 to 1806 *26*

15 North-East Africa in the 19th century *28*

16 The Atlantic slave trade and abolition in the 19th century *30*

17 West African states and economic change in the 19th century *32*

18 European Explorers and missionaries in West Africa, 1792 to 1890 *34*

19 The Mfecane in Southern, Central and Eastern Africa, c. 1818 to c. 1870 *36*

20 Trade and politics in Central and Eastern Africa, 1800 to 1890 *38*

21 European explorers and the missionary penetration of Central and Eastern Africa, 1840 to 1890 *40*

22 European expansion in Southern Africa, 1806 to 1870 *42*

23 South Africa, 1870 to 1910 *44*

24 North Africa and European imperialism, 1832 to 1936 *46*

25 West Africa and European Partition, 1875 to 1914 *48*

26 The European Partition of Central and Eastern Africa, 1875 to 1914 *50*

27 African reactions to European occupation in Eastern, Central and Southern Africa, 1880 to 1920 *52*

28 African reactions to the European occupation in West Africa, 1880 to 1920 *54*

29 Colonial boundaries in Africa, 1919 *56*

30 Economic change in North Africa during the colonial period *58*

31 Economic change in West Africa during the colonial period *60*

32 Economic change in Southern, Central and Eastern Africa during the colonial period *62*

33 South Africa, political and economic, 1910 to 1980 *64*

34 Progress to independence, 1945 to 1980 *66*

35 The new Africa *68*

36 Economic changes since independence *70*

Index *73*

1 *Physical Geography*

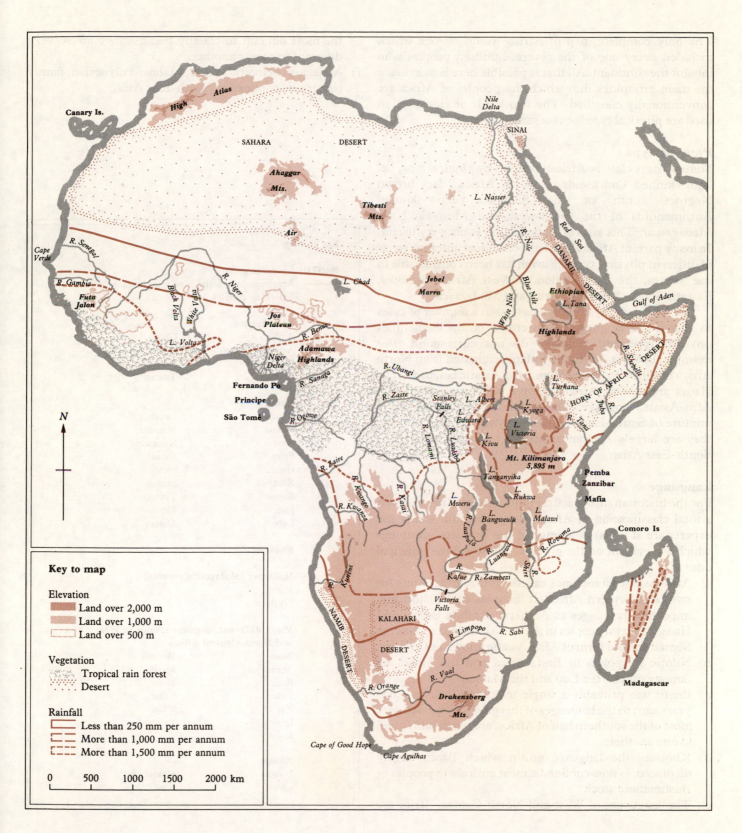

Key to map

Elevation
- Land over 2,000 m
- Land over 1,000 m
- Land over 500 m

Vegetation
- Tropical rain forest
- Desert

Rainfall
- Less than 250 mm per annum
- More than 1,000 mm per annum
- More than 1,500 mm per annum

0   500   1000   1500   2000 km

Canary Is.

High Atlas

SAHARA   DESERT

Ahaggar
Mts.

Tibesti
Mts.

Air

Cape
Verde

R. Senegal

R. Gambia

Futa
Jalon

Black Volta

White Volta

R. Niger

L. Chad

Jebel
Marra

L. Volta

Jos
Plateau

R. Benue

Niger
Delta

Adamawa
Highlands

Fernando Po

Principe

São Tomé

R. Sanaga

R. Ogowe

R. Zaire

R. Ubangi

Stanley
Falls

R. Lomami

R. Luaba

L. Albert

L. Edward

L. Kivu

Mt. Kilimanjaro
5,895 m

L.
Tanganyika

R. Zaire

R. Kwango

R. Kwanza

R. Kasai

L.
Mweru

L.
Bangweulu

L. Rukwa

L. Malawi

R. Luapula

R. Luangwa

R. Shire

R. Rovuma

R.
Kafue

R. Zambezi

Victoria
Falls

R. Cunene

NAMIB DESERT

KALAHARI

DESERT

R. Limpopo

R. Sabi

R. Vaal

R. Orange

Drakensberg
Mts.

Cape of Good Hope

Cape Agulhas

Nile
Delta

SINAI

L. Nasser

Red Sea

R. Nile

Blue Nile

White Nile

DANAKIL DESERT

Ethiopian

L. Tana

Highlands

Gulf of Aden

HORN OF AFRICA

DESERT

R. Shebelle

R. Juba

L.
Turkana

R. Tana

L.
Kyoga

L.
Victoria

L.
Rukwa

Pemba

Zanzibar

Mafia

Comoro Is

Madagascar

N

The only complete map of Africa would be one which included every one of the several hundred peoples who inhabit the continent. All that is possible here is to indicate the main groupings into which the peoples of Africa are conventionally classified. The two kinds of classification used are physical type (or race) and language.

Physical type

Some writers classify African peoples by *physical type*, i.e. light-skinned Caucasoids of North Africa; dark brown Negroes south of the Sahara; yellow-skinned Bushmanoids of the south-west and Mongoloids of Madagascar. This kind of classification is not very useful. In many parts of Africa there has been *fusion* (intermarriage) of different physical types. Fusion has been considerable in the Sahara, the Sahel region of West Africa, Ethiopia, Eastern Africa, Southern Africa and Madagascar.

The fusion of physical type has led in a number of cases to changes in language by an ethnic group. Sometimes physical type and language do not correspond. For example, in West Africa the Fulani originated from North Africa but they do not speak an Afro-Asiatic language. The Hausa are a West African people who have adopted an Afro-Asiatic language. The people of Madagascar are a mixture of South-East Asian settlers and African settlers; they are largely African in origin; but their language is South-East Asian.

Language

For the historian, the practical requirement is not so much a total classification of African languages (on which the experts are at odds) as a grasp of the language groupings which are evident on the ground. These are the principal ones:

a) Afro-Asiatic (sometimes called Erythraic) accounts for most of Northern Africa. It includes such historically important languages as Amharic, Arabic, Berber and Hausa. Several peoples in the Horn of Africa such as the Somali speak a form of Afro-Asiatic known as Cushitic.

b) Nilotic is spoken in East Africa and the Sudan by (among others) the Luo and the Maasai.

c) Bantu was probably a single tongue as little as 2,000 years ago; so the languages of this group, dispersed over most of the southern half of Africa, are remarkably close to one another.

d) Khoisan, the language group which Bantu largely displaced, is now confined almost entirely to peoples of Bushmanoid stock.

e) The languages of West and North-Central Africa are the most difficult to classify because they are so very different from one another.

f) Malagasy belongs to the Malayo-Polynesian family (otherwise confined to South-East Asia).

Key to map

BANTU	Language group
———	Approximate boundaries of main language groups
YAO	Individual peoples

Afro-Asiatic

Amhara	Galla
Arabs	Hausa
Beja	Somali
Berbers	Tuareg

Bantu

Bemba	Lunda
Cokwe	Mbundu
Herero	Nyamwezi
Fang	Shona
Ganda	Sotho
Kikuyu	Swahili
Kongo	Tswana
Lozi	Yao
Luba	Xhosa

Khoisan

Malagasy (Malayo-Polynesian)

Merina
Sakalava

Many different language groups in West and North-Central Africa

Akan	Malinke
Azande	Mende
Banda	Mossi
Fulani	Nuba
Fur	Wolof
Igbo	Yoruba
Kanuri	

Nilotic

Dinka	Maasai
Luo	Nuer

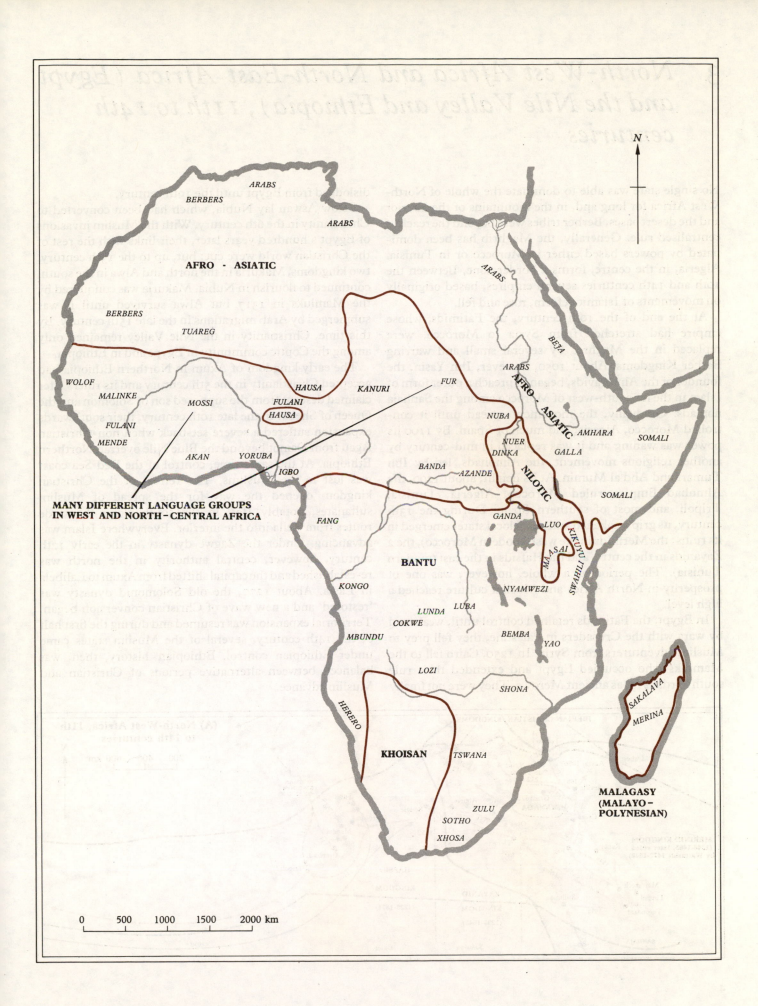

3 North-West Africa and North-East Africa (Egypt and the Nile Valley and Ethiopia), 11th to 14th centuries

No single state was able to dominate the whole of North-West Africa for long and, in the mountains of the interior and the desert oases, Berber tribes were beyond the reach of centralised rule. Generally, the Maghrib has been dominated by powers based either in Morocco or in Tunisia. Algeria, in the centre, forms a border zone. Between the 10th and 14th centuries several empires, based originally on movements of Islamic reform, rose and fell.

At the end of the 10th century, the Fatimids, whose empire had stretched from Syria to Morocco, were replaced in the Maghrib by several small and warring Berber Kingdoms. About 1050, however, Ibn Yasin, the founder of the Almoravids, began to preach a purer form of Islam in the far south-west of Morocco among the Sanhaja nomads. Gradually, the movement spread until it controlled Morocco, Algeria, and much of Spain. By 1100 its power was waning and it was replaced in mid-century by another religious movement, the Almohads, led by Ibn Tumart and Abd al Mumin. At its height, about 1200, the Almohad Empire ruled Morocco, Algeria, Tunisia, Tripoli, and most of southern Spain. During the 13th century, its grip weakened and small local states emerged in its ruins: the Merinids in the west (modern Morocco), the 2 Zayanids in the centre, and the Hafsids in the east (modern Tunisia). The period as a whole, however, was one of prosperity in North Africa and Muslim culture reached a high level.

In Egypt, the Fatimids retained control until, weakened by wars with the Crusaders in Palestine, they fell prey to Muslim adventurers from Syria. In 1250, Cairo fell to the Mamluks who occupied Egypt and extended their rule southwards as far as ancient Merowe. They were not finally dislodged from Egypt until the 19th century.

Below Aswan lay Nubia, which had been converted to Christianity in the 6th century. With the Muslim invasions of Egypt a hundred years later, their links with the rest of the Christian world were cut; but, up to the 13th century, two kingdoms, Makuria in the north and Alwa in the south, continued to flourish in Nubia. Makuria was conquered by the Mamluks in 1317 but Alwa survived until it was submerged by Arab migrations in the late 15th century. By this time, Christianity in the Nile Valley remained only among the Coptic community in Egypt and in Ethiopia.

The early kingdom of Axum in Northern Ethiopia had accepted Christianity in the 5th century and its rulers later claimed descent from the supposed son of Solomon and the Queen of Sheba. In the late 10th century, their southwards expansion suffered a severe set-back when non-Christian Agau from Damot beyond the Blue Nile overran Northern Ethiopia. At the same time, control of the Red Sea coast was lost to the Muslims. The retreat of the Christian kingdom opened the way for the spread of Muslim sultanates, notably Ifat, in the south along the trade routes from Zeila into the interior. Everywhere Islam was advancing. Under the Zagwe dynasty in the early 12th century, however, central authority in the north was re-established and the capital shifted from Axum to Lalibela in Lasta. About 1270, the old Solomonid dynasty was 'restored' and a new wave of Christian conversion began. Territorial expansion was resumed and during the first half of the 14th century, several of the Muslim states came under Ethiopian control. Ethiopian history, then, was balanced between alternative periods of Christian and Muslim advance.

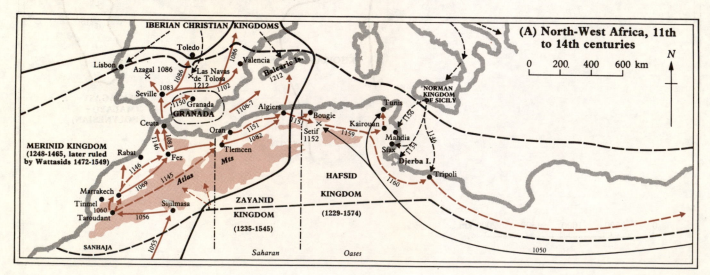

(A) North-West Africa, 11th to 14th centuries

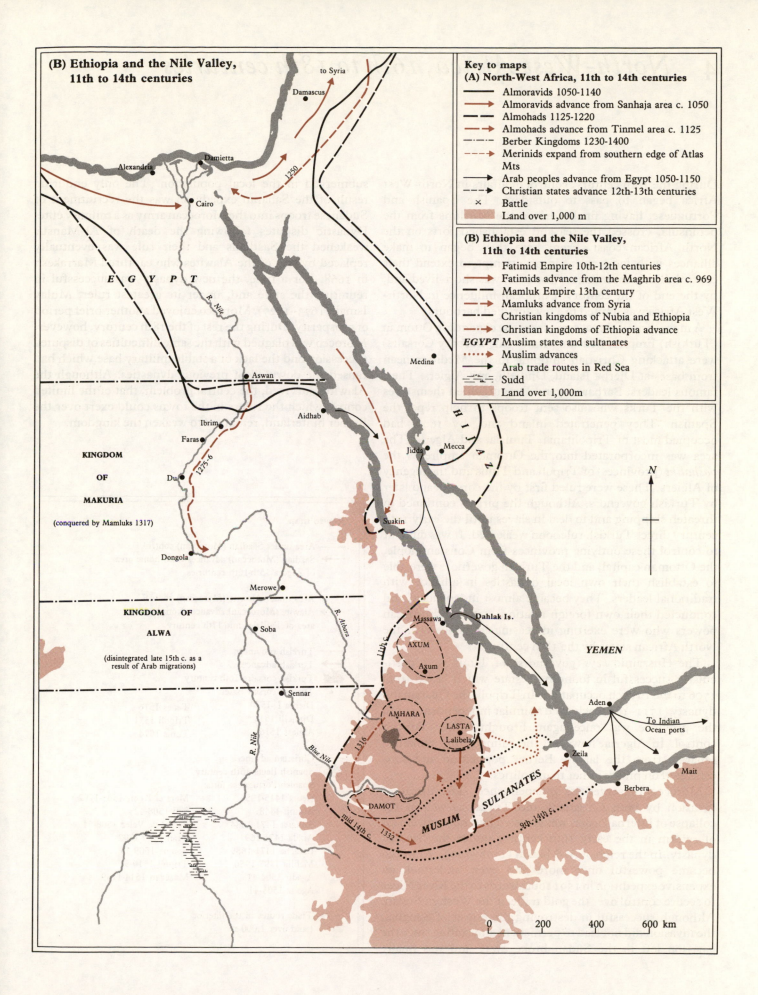

(B) Ethiopia and the Nile Valley, 11th to 14th centuries

to Syria

Damascus

Alexandria

Damietta

Cairo

EGYPT

R. Nile

1250

Aswan

Medina

Ibrim

Aidhab

Faras

Jidda

Mecca

KINGDOM

Du

1275-6

OF

H I J A Z

MAKURIA

(conquered by Mamluks 1317)

Dongola

Merowe

KINGDOM OF

ALWA

Soba

R. Athara

(disintegrated late 15th c. as a
result of Arab migrations)

Suakin

Sennar

R. Nile

Massawa

Dahlak Is.

11th c.

AXUM

Axum

YEMEN

Aden

Blue Nile

AMHARA

LASTA

Lalibela

To Indian
Ocean ports

1316

DAMOT

MUSLIM **SULTANATES**

Zeila

Mait

9th-14th c.

Berbera

mid 14th c.

1332

N

0   200   400   600 km

Key to maps

(A) North-West Africa, 11th to 14th centuries

————— Almoravids 1050-1140
——▶ Almoravids advance from Sanhaja area c. 1050
– – – Almohads 1125-1220
– –▶ Almohads advance from Tinmel area c. 1125
–·–·– Berber Kingdoms 1230-1400
– · –▶ Merinids expand from southern edge of Atlas Mts
——▶ Arab peoples advance from Egypt 1050-1150
– – –▶ Christian states advance 12th-13th centuries
× Battle
▨ Land over 1,000 m

(B) Ethiopia and the Nile Valley, 11th to 14th centuries

————— Fatimid Empire 10th-12th centuries
——▶ Fatimids advance from the Maghrib area c. 969
– – – Mamluk Empire 13th century
– –▶ Mamluks advance from Syria
–·–·– Christian kingdoms of Nubia and Ethiopia
– · –▶ Christian kingdoms of Ethiopia advance
EGYPT Muslim states and sultanates
········▶ Muslim advances
➡ Arab trade routes in Red Sea
▨ Sudd
▨ Land over 1,000m

North-West Africa, 16th to 18th centuries

During the 16th century, control of affairs in North-West Africa began to pass to outsiders. The Spanish and Portuguese, having finally driven the Muslims from the peninsula, crossed the sea and established forts on the North African coast. From here they began to make alliances with local rulers in an attempt to extend their control. Their ascendancy, however, was short-lived and, by the end of the century, European influence in North-West Africa was limited to a few fortified harbours.

A more serious threat came from the expanding Ottoman (Turkish) Empire. Muslim pirates (the Barbary Corsairs) were attacking Christian shipping in the Mediterranean from bases at Djerba Island, Djidjelli, and Algiers. Their famous leaders, Barbarossa and Dragut, allied themselves with the Turks who also sent troops to help repel the Spanish. They penetrated inland and, by 1600, had occupied most of Tripolitania, Tunisia, and Algeria. The area was incorporated into the Ottoman empire as the *pashaliks* (provinces) of Tripoli and Tunis and the regency of Algiers. These were ruled first by the corsairs and later by Turkish governors. Although the pirates continued to threaten shipping and to deal in slaves until the early 19th century direct Turkish rule soon weakened. It was difficult to control these outlying provinces from Constantinople, the Ottoman capital, and the Turkish governors were able to establish their own local dynasties in alliance with traditional leaders. They became almost independent and conducted their own foreign relations with the European powers who were exerting increasing influence over the North African states by the 18th century.

The Hussainid *beys* (governors) of Tunis were particularly successful in founding a state which lasted from 1706 to the French occupation. In Tripoli, the Quaramanli dynasty (1711–1835) achieved a similar independence until the province was once again brought under Turkish control. In Algeria, however, the ruling group remained separate from the largely Berber population and concentrated on piracy rather than politics.

Morocco preserved its independence. The threat of invasion by both Christians and Turks, as well as the collapse of internal order, was arrested by a new movement of reform in the early 16th century under the Saadian dynasty. In the reign of Al-Mansur (1578–1603), Morocco became powerful once more and even undertook an expensive expedition in 1591 southwards to the River Niger to secure control over the gold trade of the Western Sudan. Although successful in destroying the power of Songhai, the invasion did not lead to permanent annexation since the garrison left in the Sudan broke away and was finally submerged in the local population. The only enduring result of the Saharan expedition was the recruitment of Sudanese troops into the Moroccan army as a military elite. Dynastic disputes following the death of Al-Mansur weakened the Saadians and their rule was eventually replaced by that of the Alawites who captured Marrakesh in 1668. For a time, the new dynasty was successful in reuniting the state and, under its greatest ruler, Mulay Ismail (1673–1727), Morocco enjoyed another brief period of prosperity. During the rest of the 18th century, however, Morocco was plagued with the same difficulties of disputed succession and the lack of a stable military base which had caused the downfall of previous dynasties. Although the Alawites survived, the central problem, that of the limited control which the rulers in the towns could exert over the Berber hinterland, remained to weaken the kingdom.

Key to map

––– Area under Saadian (Moroccan) control

→ Saadian (Moroccan) advances from home area of Zagora 15th-16th centuries

///// Area under Alawite (Moroccan) control

·····► Alawite (Moroccan) advances from home area of Tafilalet mid 17th century

––– Turkish provinces

→ Turkish advances

⛵ Turkish corsairs 16th century

▲ Turkish corsair bases:

Djerba I. 1510	Tenes 1516
Djidjelli 1514	Tripoli 1551
Algiers 1516	Tunis 1574

→ Christian advances

⛵ Spanish fleets 16th century

■ Spanish/Portuguese forts:

Ceuta 1415-1956	Mers el Kebir 1505-1792
Arguin 1448	Safi 1508-42
Tangier 1471-1684	Penon de Velez 1508-54
Arzila 1471-1691	Oran 1509-1792
Larache 1471-1689	Bougie 1509-55
Melilla 1497-1956	Tripoli 1510-51
Agadir 1504-41	Mazagan 1514-1769
Agouz 1505-41	

→ Trade routes in the interior

▬ Land over 1,000 m

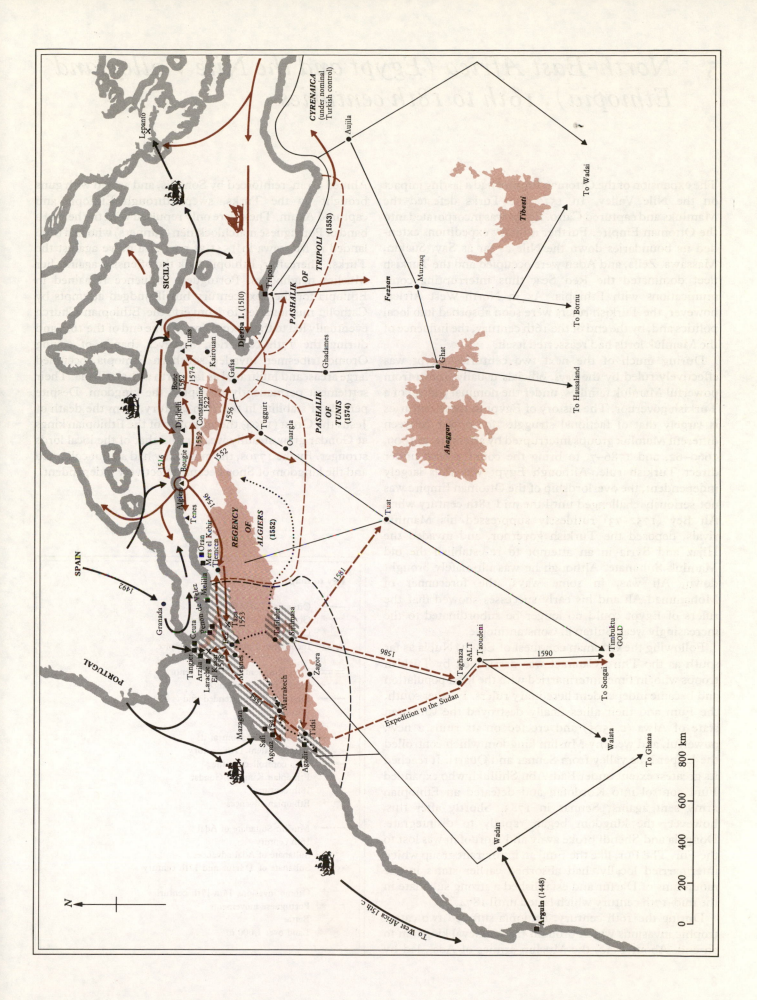

5 North-East Africa (Egypt and the Nile Valley and Ethiopia), 16th to 18th centuries

The expansion of the Ottoman Empire had a lasting impact on the Nile Valley. In 1517 the Turks defeated the Mamluks and captured Cairo. Egypt was incorporated into the Ottoman Empire. Further military expeditions extended its boundaries down the Nile as far as Say. Suakin, Massawa, Zeila, and Aden were occupied and the Turkish fleet dominated the Red Sea, thus interrupting communications with Ethiopia. As in North-West Africa, however, the Turkish rulers were soon absorbed into local politics and, by the end of the 16th century, the influence of the Mamluk lords had reasserted itself.

During much of the next two centuries Egypt was effectively ruled by the *beys*, officials usually drawn from powerful Mamluk families, under the nominal control of a Turkish governor. The history of Egypt in these centuries is largely that of factional struggles for power between different Mamluk groups interrupted by attempts, in 1609, 1660–62, and 1786–7, to bring the country back under direct Turkish rule. Although Egypt was thus largely independent, the overlordship of the Ottoman Empire was not seriously challenged until the mid 18th century when Ali Bey (1752–73) ruthlessly suppressed his Mamluk rivals, deposed the Turkish governor, and invaded the Hijaz and Syria in an attempt to re-establish the old Mamluk Sultanate. Although he was ultimately brought down, Ali was, in some ways, the forerunner of Mohammed Ali and his early successes showed that the rulers of Egypt could no longer be subordinated to the increasingly weak Sultan in Constantinople.

Following the Ottoman conquest of Egypt, Nubia as far south as the Third Cataract was garrisoned by Turkish troops who, in time, intermarried with the local population and became independent hereditary rulers. Further south, the Funj and their allies finally destroyed the Christian state of Alwa (c.1505) and erected on its ruins a new, powerful, and wealthy Muslim kingdom which controlled the Upper Nile valley from Sennar and Quarri. It reached its greatest extent under Badi Abu Shillukh who expanded Funj control into Kordofan and defeated an Ethiopian army sent against Sennar in 1783. Shortly after this, however, the kingdom began rapidly to disintegrate. Dongola and Shendi broke away and Kordofan was lost to the Fur. The Fur, like the Funj an immigrant group which intermarried locally, had absorbed earlier states in the mountains of Darfur and established a strong sultanate in the mid-17th century which lasted until 1874.

During the 16th century, Ethiopia suffered two catastrophic invasions which brought the medieval kingdom to an end. About 1530, the Muslim armies of Adal, led by Ahmed Gran, reinforced by Somalis, and armed with guns brought by the Turks, swept through Ethiopia and captured Axum. They were only repulsed with the help of a band of Portuguese matchlockmen (gunners) who had been landed at Massawa in 1541 as part of a move against the Turks. Thereafter, Ethiopia took the offensive against her Muslim neighbours. Portuguese influence remained in Ethiopia for the next century but ill-judged attempts by Catholic missionaries to 'convert' the Ethiopian Church eventually led to their expulsion. At the end of the 16th and during the 17th centuries, however, bands of roving Oromo tribesmen invaded southern Ethiopia, occupied large areas, and infiltrated as far north as Lake Tana. Their settlement permanently disrupted the kingdom. Despite periods of stability in the 17th century, from the death of Jesus the Great (1704) the authority of the Ethiopian kings at Gondar grew steadily weaker and that of the local lords stronger. By the 1770s, the monarchy had all but collapsed and the kingdom of Shoa became effectively independent.

Key to map

——	Ottoman (Turkish) Empire
→	Ottoman (Turkish) advances
⛵	Ottoman (Turkish) navy
HIJAZ	Incorporated into Ottoman Empire
===	Funj Kingdom early 16th century
→→	Funj Kingdom advances
——	Funj Kingdom extended mid 17th century
—·—	Ethiopian Kingdom at its greatest extent 17th century
-----	Area controlled by the Ethiopian Kings of Gondar 18th century
--→	Ethiopian advances
—··—	Muslim Sultanate of Adal 16th century
--→	Sultanate of Adal advances
·····	Sultanate of Darfur mid 17th century
--→	Oromo invasions 16th-17th centuries
--→	Portuguese movements
×	Battle
▧	Land over 1,000 m

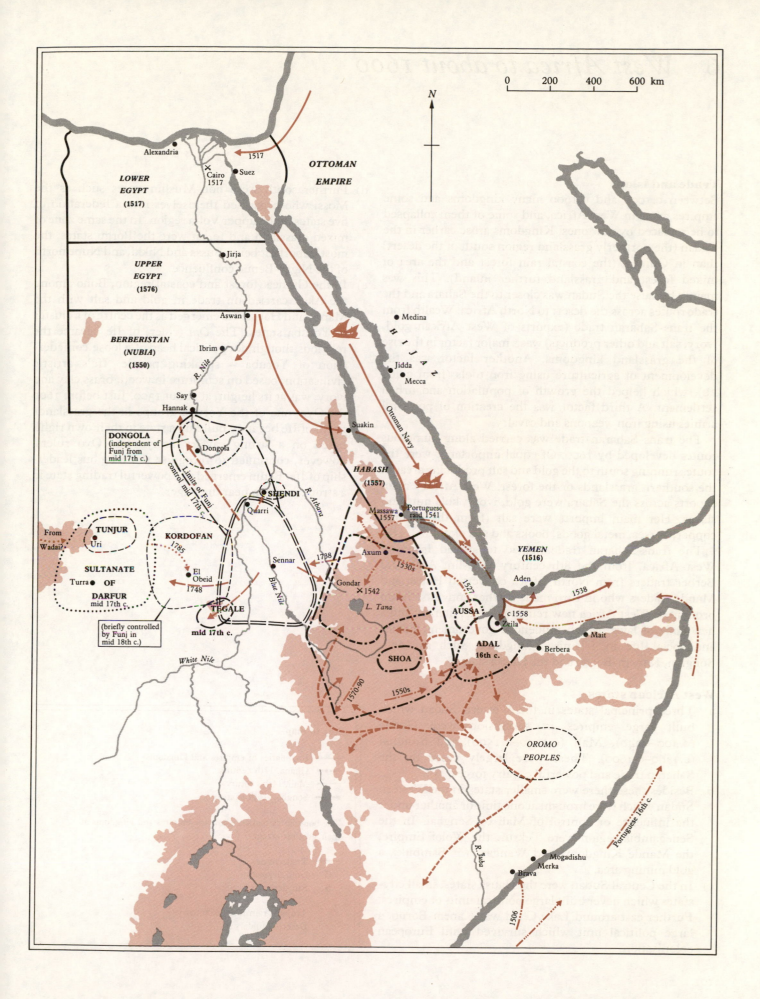

0   200   400   600 km

N

Alexandria
Cairo
1517
Suez

1517

OTTOMAN
EMPIRE

LOWER
EGYPT
(1517)

Jirja

UPPER
EGYPT
(1576)

Medina

HIJAZ

Jidda
Mecca

Aswan

Ibrim

BERBERISTAN
(NUBIA)
(1550)

R. Nile

Ottoman Navy

Say
Hannak

Suakin

DONGOLA
(independent of
Funj from
mid 17th c.)

Dongola

HABASH
(1557)

Limits of Funj
control mid 17th c.

SHENDI
Quarri

R. Atbara

Massawa   Portuguese
1557   raid 1541

From
Wadai?

TUNJUR
Uri

KORDOFAN
1785

SULTANATE
Turra   OF

El
Obeid
1748

DARFUR
mid 17th c.

(briefly controlled
by Funj in
mid 18th c.)

Sennar

Blue Nile

1738

Axum

1530s

Gondar
×1542

L. Tana

1527

YEMEN
(1516)

Aden

1538

c 1558
Zeila

Mait

AUSSA

ADAL
16th c.

Berbera

TEGALE
mid 17th c.

White Nile

SHOA

1570-90   1550s

OROMO
PEOPLES

R. Juba

Portuguese 16th c.

Mogadishu
Merka
Brava

1506

6 West Africa to about 1600

Trade and Islam

Between c.1000 and c.1600 many kingdoms and some empires arose in West Africa, and some of them collapsed to be replaced by new ones. Kingdoms arose earlier in the Sudan (the northerly grassland region south of the desert) than in Guinea, (the coastal rain forest and the area of mixed forest and grassland further inland). This was mainly because the Sudan was closer to the Sahara and the trade routes across the desert to North Africa. Wealth from the trans-Saharan trade (exports of West African gold, ivory, salt and other products) was a major factor in the rise of the grassland kingdoms. Another factor was the development of agriculture using iron tools (from c.400 BC), which helped the growth of population and urban settlement. A third factor was the creation of powerful armies using iron weapons and cavalry.

The trans-Saharan trade was carried along numerous routes developed by 1600. Of equal importance were the routes running south to the gold and salt producing areas in the southern grasslands or the forest. West Africa's main exports across the Sahara were gold, ivory, kola nuts and slaves. Her main imports were salt (from the desert), copper, horses, metal goods, books and silk clothes.

The trans-Saharan trade helped to spread Islam to West Africa, from the 8th century. Muslim Arab and Berber traders from North Africa converted Hausa and Mande traders who in turn made further converts. Islam brought to West Africa new religious ideas, literacy and a new code of laws, which influenced government, justice and social life in Islamised kingdoms such as Mali, Songhai, Kanem-Borno and the Hausa states.

West African states

a) Three principal states in the Western Sudan which built large empires in succession were Ghana (c.400–1240), Mali (c.1240–c.1500) and Songhai (c.1460–c.1600). These were largely based on the Saharan trade and powerful cavalry forces.

b) Besides these there were smaller states in the Western Sudan which were brought at one time or another under the influence or control of Mali or Songhai. In the Senegambia region were Tekrur, the Wolof Empire, the Mande Kingdoms and Wangara (or Bambuk), a gold mining area.

c) In the Central Sudan were the Hausa states, small city-states which never built large political units or empires. Further east around Lake Chad was Kanem-Borno, a large political unit which survived until European colonisation.

d) Further south were non-Muslim states such as the Mossi who organised themselves into a federation of five states in the upper Volta region. In the same zone of mixed grassland and forest were the Borgu states, the most important being Bussa and Nikki, and Nupe north of the Niger-Benue confluence.

e) In the Guinea (forest and coastal) region, Bono among the Akan carried on trade in gold and salt with the Mande and Hausa. Ife emerged as the centre of a cluster of Yoruba states. The *Oni* (ruler) of Ife became the religious though not political head of a loose confederation of Yoruba – speaking people. Ife's artistic civilisation, based on sculpture in wood, brass clay and ivory, was at its height, at about 1300. Just before 1600 the Oyo, one of the Yoruba groups in the grasslands north of Ife began to build up a state in their own right, based on a strong cavalry army. The Oyo rulers, however, continued to recognise the religious leadership of Ife. Benin emerged as a powerful trading state in a strong position near the Niger.

Key to map

——— Boundaries of empires and kingdoms
•••••• Ghana, 11th century
– – – Mali, 14th century
— — Songhai, 16th century

The boundaries marked show the empires and kingdoms at their greatest extent.

→ Trade routes
G Gold deposits
S Salt deposits

Tropical rain forest boundary
Desert boundary

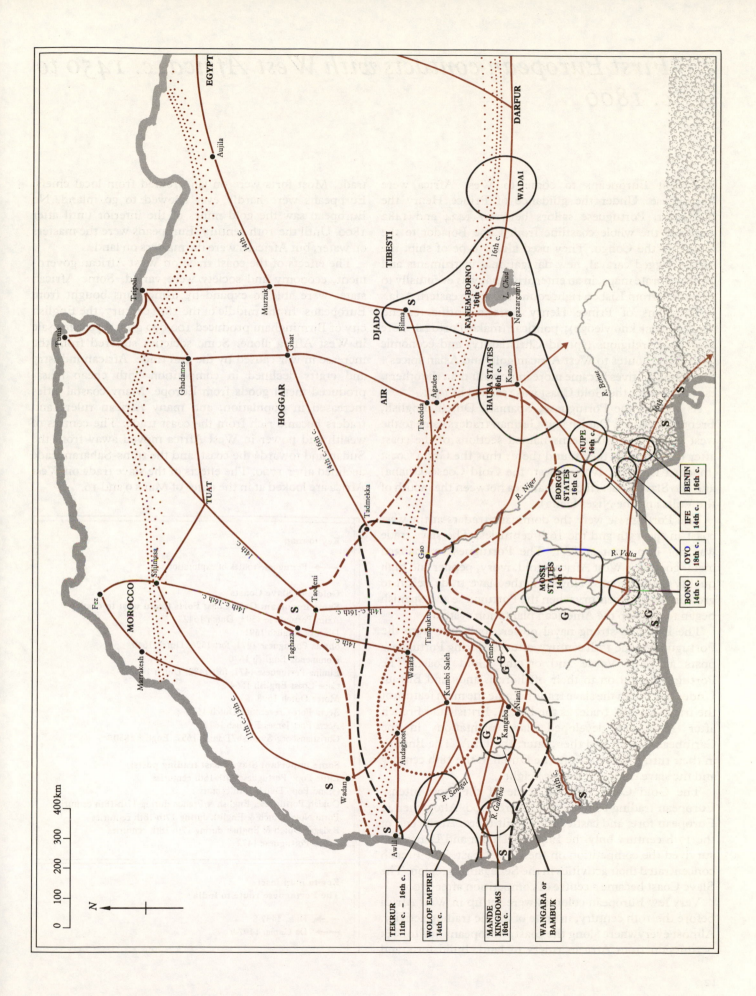

EGYPT

DARFUR

WADAI
16th c.

TIBESTI

KANEM-BORNO
16th c.

L. Chad

Ngazargamu

DJADO

Bilma S

AIR

HAUSA STATES
16th c.
Kano

R. Benue

Agades

Takedda

Aujila

Tripoli

14th c.

Murzuk

Tunis

Ghadames

Ghat

HOGGAR

14th c.-16th c.

TUAT

Tadmekka

Gao

R. Niger

NUPE
16th c.

BORGU
STATES
16th c.

BENIN
16th c.

IFE
14th c.

OYO
18th c.

Sijilmasa

14th c.

Taodeni

14th c.-16th c.

R. Volta

MOSSI
STATES
14th c.

G

BONO
14th c.

MOROCCO

Fez

Marrakesh

11th c.-13th c.

Taghaza

14th c.

Walata

Timbuktu

Jenne

G
G

G

S
S

Kumbi Saleh

Niani

G Kangaba

14th c.

Audaghost

R. Senegal

G

S

R. Gambia

S

Wadan

400 km

0 100 200 300

N

Awlil

S

TEKRUR
11th c. – 16th c.

WOLOF EMPIRE
14th c.

MANDE
KINGDOMS
16th c.

WANGARA or
BAMBUK

7 First European contacts with West Africa, c. 1450 to c. 1800

The first Europeans to come to West Africa were Portuguese. Under the guidance of Prince Henry the Navigator, Portuguese sailors between 1434 and 1482 explored the whole coastline from Cape Bojador to the mouth of the Congo. They used a new type of ship, the square-rigged caraval, new navigational instruments and more accurate maps, in an enterprise that was eventually to take them from Lisbon right round Africa to eastern Asia.

The aims of Prince Henry were scientific (extend geographical knowledge); political (make Portugal more powerful); religious (spread Christianity) and economic (find direct routes to West African gold and Asian spices). Economic motives became more important than the others, especially after the Gold Coast was reached in 1471.

As well as the Portuguese, Spanish, Dutch, English, French, Swedish, Danish and German traders came to the west coast. The Europeans named sections of the coast after the products they found there: thus the Grain Coast (modern Liberia), Ivory Coast, the Gold Coast (Ghana) and the Slave Coast (the coastal area between the mouth of the Volta and the Niger Delta).

The Portuguese were the dominant traders at the west coast in the 15th and the 16th centuries. The slave trade was not important at first. The Portuguese exchanged metal goods for West African gold, ivory, pepper and high quality cotton goods. However, the slave trade began to grow in the 16th century when the Portuguese and Spanish began to develop the American plantation system.

The Dutch, a strong naval power, took over from the Portuguese in the 17th century, after capturing Portuguese posts at Cape Verde and on the Gold Coast. The Portuguese held on to their offshore islands and Bissau. Under the Dutch the slave trade became the main feature of the trans-Atlantic trade, as the Dutch, British and French after 1650 also developed slave plantations in the Caribbean islands and then, later, the USA. The English in their turn took over from the Dutch in the 18th century and the slave trade reached its height.

The Gold Coast was the scene of the most intense European trading competition before 1700. Altogether 41 European forts and castles were built there. At the end of the 17th century only the English, Dutch and Danes had survived the competition on the Gold Coast. The French concentrated their activities in the Senegambia region. The Slave Coast became a centre of competition after 1700.

Very few European colonies were set up in West Africa before the 19th century, in spite of all the trading activity. Almost everywhere along the coast, Europeans had to seek permission from African rulers to land, build forts and trade. Most forts were on land rented from local chiefs. Europeans were hardly ever allowed to go inland. No European saw the gold mines of the interior until after 1800. Until the 19th century, Europeans were the masters on water, but Africans were the masters on land.

The effects of the coast trade on West African government, economy and society were varied. Some African states were able to expand by using guns bought from Europeans. In the middle of the 18th century, the English city of Birmingham produced 100,000 guns a year for sale in West Africa alone. Some societies suffered from the increase in war caused by the gun trade. African industry and crafts declined in competition with cheap mass-produced metal goods from Europe. Many coastal cities increased in population, and many African rulers and traders became rich from the coast trade. The centres of wealth and power in West Africa moved away from the Sudan and towards the coast, and the trans-Saharan trade declined after 1700. The effects of the slave trade on West Africa are looked at in the notes of Maps 9 and 16.

Key to map

→ Portuguese routes of exploration

Gold and Slave Coasts
Some important Gold Coast Forts (from west to east):
Axim Portuguese 1503; Dutch 1642
Dixcove English 1691
Shama Portuguese 1471, fort 1526; Dutch 1640
Kommenda English 1670
Elmina Portuguese 1471, fort 1482; Dutch 1637
Cape Coast English 1664
Moree Dutch 1598
Accra Fort Crevecouer Dutch 1650
Accra Fort James English 1673
Christiansborg Swedish/Danish 1657; English 1850

Some important Slave Coast trading posts:
Little Popo Portuguese 17th-18th centuries
Grand Popo Dutch 17th century
Ouidah Portuguese, English & French during 17th-18th centuries
Porto Novo Dutch & English during 17th-18th centuries
Badagry Dutch & English during 17th-18th centuries
Lagos Portuguese 1472

Key to map inset
The Portuguese route to India

→ Dias, 1487-8
→ Da Gama, 1497-9

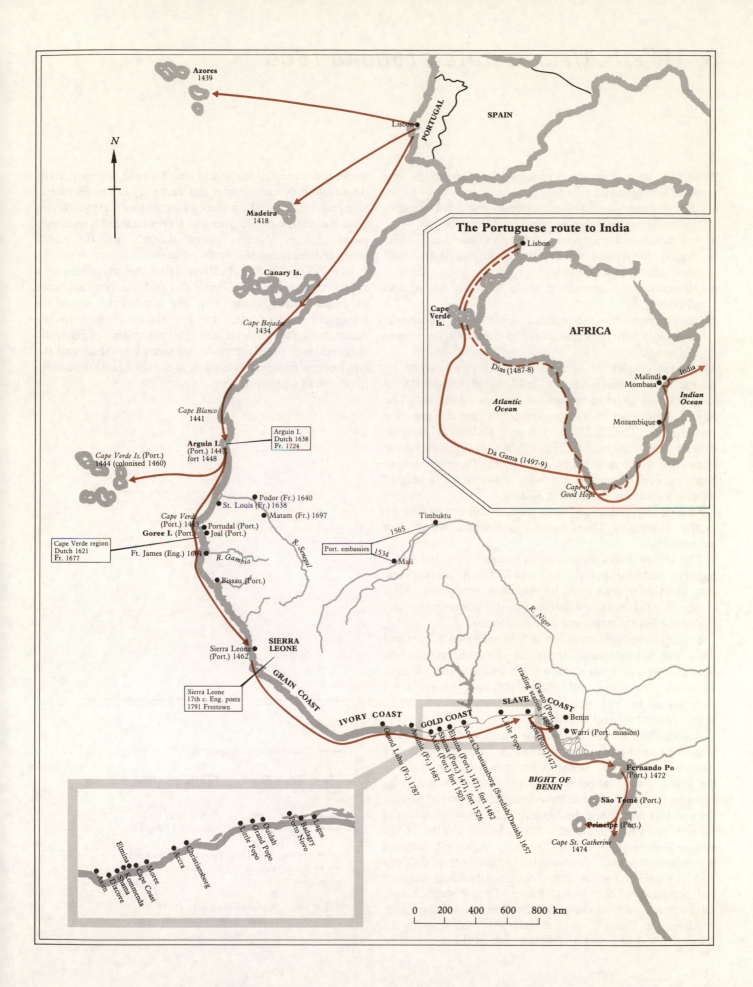

The Portuguese route to India

Lisbon

Cape Verde Is.

AFRICA

Dias (1487-8)

Atlantic Ocean

Da Gama (1497-9)

Cape of Good Hope

Malindi
Mombasa
Mozambique

India

Indian Ocean

Azores
1439

PORTUGAL

SPAIN

Lisbon

N

Madeira
1418

Canary Is.

Cape Bojador
1434

Cape Blanco
1441

Arguin I.
(Port.) 1443
fort 1448

Arguin I.
Dutch 1638
Fr. 1724

Cape Verde Is. (Port.)
1444 (colonised 1460)

Cape Verde
(Port.) 1445
Goree I. (Port.)

Cape Verde region
Dutch 1621
Fr. 1677

Portudal (Port.)
Joal (Port.)

Ft. James (Eng.) 1664

Podor (Fr.) 1640
St. Louis (Fr.) 1638
Matam (Fr.) 1697

R. Senegal

R. Gambia

Bissau (Port.)

Timbuktu

Port. embassies

1565

1534

Mali

R. Niger

Sierra Leone
(Port.) 1462

SIERRA
LEONE

Sierra Leone
17th c. Eng. posts
1791 Freetown

GRAIN COAST

IVORY COAST

GOLD COAST

SLAVE COAST

Grand Lahu

Assinie (Fr.) 1687

Axim (Port.) fort 1503
Shama (Port.) 1471
Elmina (Port.) 1471, fort 1482
Accra

Christiansborg (Swedish/Danish) 1657

Little Popo

Gwato (Port.)
trading station 1486

Lagos (Port.) 1472

Benin

Warri (Port. mission)

Fernando Po
(Port.) 1472

BIGHT OF
BENIN

São Tomé (Port.)

Principe (Port.)

Cape St. Catherine
1474

Akin
Dixcove
Shama
Kommenda
Cape Coast
Elmina
Moree
Accra
Christiansborg
Little Popo
Grand Popo
Ouidah
Porto Novo
Badagry
Lagos

0   200   400   600   800 km

8 West African states, 1600 to 1800

After 1600 many new states emerged in West Africa, as a result of several factors:

a) The collapse or decline of Sudanic (grassland) empires and their replacement by new kingdoms;

b) the continued migration of peoples into the Guinea region (the coastal rain forest and the mixed grassland and forest further inland);

c) the continued growth of trade between Sudan and Guinea;

d) the increase in the coastal trade with Europeans especially with the expansion of the Atlantic slave trade after 1650.

The great empire of Songhai was overrun in 1591 by Moroccan invaders in search of gold. Songhai resisted for a long time but by 1650 the empire had ceased to exist. The Niger cities were now unprotected in the absence of a strong state. The Wallimunden and Tadmekkei Tuareg won control of the middle Niger (1680–1740) while on the upper Niger Songhai was replaced by the Bambara state of Segu, which expanded 1710–50. After 1750 a second Bambara state was founded in Kaarta.

Kanem-Borno declined after 1660, losing much territory to the Tuareg of Takedda and to Bagirmi which won independence.

The Hausa states continued to flourish from the trans-Saharan trade through Air to Tripoli. To the south, Nupe continued to benefit from its middleman position. After c. 1600 the Jukun state expanded in the Benue valley and raided the Hausa states and Kanem-Borno.

Several new states arose in the Senegal basin: Cayor and Baol, which broke away from the Wolof Empire in the Senegambia, and Futa Toro, a multi-ethnic state of Wolof, Tokolor, Mandinka and Fulani. Muslim governments were set up by Fulani reformers in Futa Jalon (c. 1725), Futa Toro (1776) and Bondu (1770s).

Among the Akan of present-day southern Ghana several important gold trading states arose, to succeed the earlier Akan state of Bono. Akwamu expanded eastwards across the Volta to the Dahomey coast 1670–1710. In the 1730s Akwamu was supplanted by Akyem. Meanwhile Asante, the greatest Akan state, had emerged as a confederation of states around Kumase from c. 1690. Asante created a large empire between 1700 and 1824, conquering hitherto powerful states such as Denkyira to the south and Gonja and Dagomba to the north, and continually threatening the independence of the coastal Fante. To the west, Asante migrants after 1750 founded the Baule and Anyi states.

Along the 'Slave Coast', Allada (Ardrah) arose in the 1600s around the port of Ouidah, but in the 1700s came under the control of the inland kingdom of Dahomey. In its turn Dahomey came under the authority of the empire of Oyo, which reached its peak of expansion c. 1750. Oyo's wealth in cotton production and slaves enabled it to absorb many smaller Yoruba states, though not Ife which remained the focus of Yoruba religion.

In the Niger and Cross River deltas the city-states such as Brass, New Calabar, Bonny and Old Calabar continued to expand their trade with the hinterland to satisfy European traders' demand for slaves to sell in the Americas. In the interior, the Igbo communities generally suffered from the slave trade but some like Aboh and the Aro became prosperous from it, as did the Igala kingdom to the north of Igboland.

Key to map

—— Boundaries and kingdoms

The boundaries marked show the empires and kingdoms at their greatest extent

⟶ Moroccan invasion of Songhai in 1591

┈⟶ Wallimunden and Tadmekkei Tuareg raids on Gao and Timbuktu

─⟶ Tuareg of Takedda raids on Kanem-Borno

╌⟶ Jukun raids

┅⟶ Bagirmi revolt

⋯⋯ Southern edge of the Sahara Desert

Northern edge of the tropical rain forest

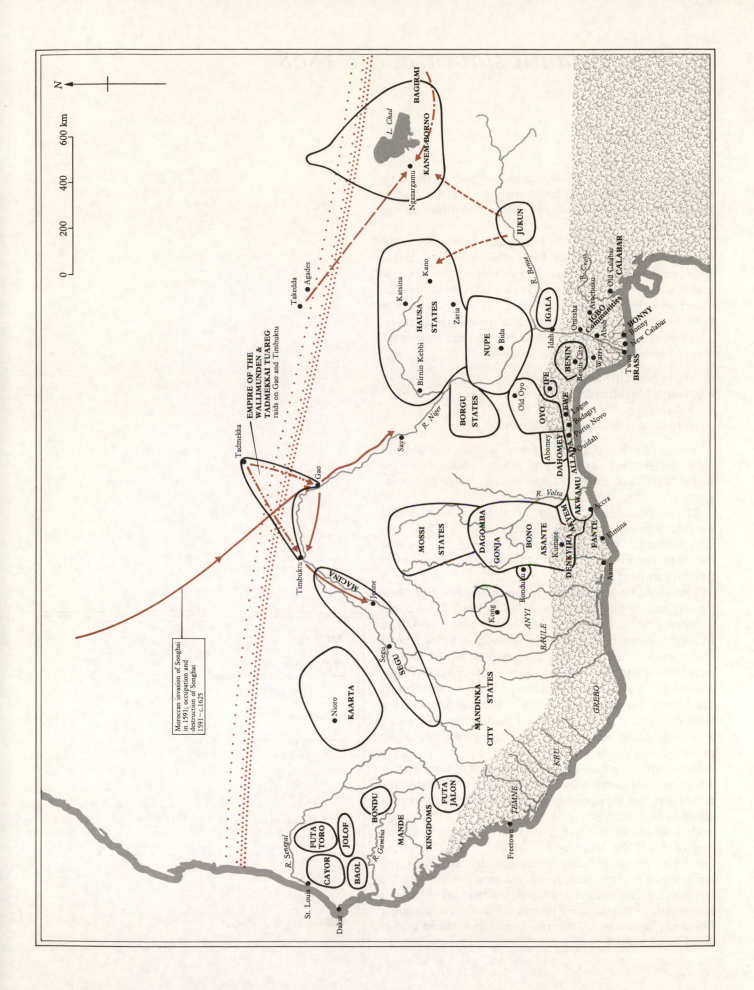

N

600 km
400
200
0

L. Chad

BAGIRMI

KANEM–BORNO

Nguzargamu

JUKUN

Agades

Takedda

R. Benue

Kano

Katsina

HAUSA
STATES

Zaria

NUPE

Bida

Birnin Kebbi

EMPIRE OF THE
WALLIMUNDEN &
TADMEKKAI TUAREG
raids on Gao and Timbuktu

IGALA

Omitsha
Arechuku
Aboh
Old Calabar
CALABAR
R. Cross
IGBO
Communities
Idah

BENIN
Benin City

BONNY
New Calabar

Warri

Twon
BRASS

Tadmekka

BORGU
STATES

Old Oyo

IFE

OYO

EWE

Lagos

Abomey
DAHOMEY

Badagry
Porto Novo

ALLADA

Ouidah

AKWAMU
AKYEM

DENKYIRA

FANTE
Accra
Elmina

Axim

R. Niger

Say

Gao

R. Volta

MOSSI
STATES

DAGOMBA

GONJA

BONO
ASANTE
Kumase

MACINA

Jenne

Timbuktu

Bondulu

Koong

ANYI

BAULE

GREBO

Moroccan invasion of Songhai
in 1591; occupation and
destruction of Songhai
1591–c.1625

Segu

SEGU

Nioro

KAARTA

MANDINKA
CITY
STATES

KRU

R. Senegal

FUTA
TORO

JOLOF

BONDU

R. Gambia

FUTA
JALON

MANDE
KINGDOMS

TEMNE

Freetown

CAVOR

BAOL

St. Louis

Dakar

9   The Atlantic slave trade to 1808

We saw in Map 7 that slaves replaced gold as the main export in the West Coast trade after 1650, as the Dutch, British and French developed large plantations in the Americas.

After the expulsion of the Portuguese from most of the West African coast, many forts were built by various European trading nations. These forts were built as residences for trade officials, and as warehouses to store the slaves and their imported commodities. They were also built as defensive bases to protect their interests in the trade.

Four main methods of obtaining slaves were used on the West Coast:

a) slaves taken in inter-state wars;
b) raiding for slaves;
c) kidnapping;
d) convicted criminals sold as slaves.

The price of a slave depended on age, size, sex and demand for slaves. At the end of the 18th century young men were bought for £26 on the West Coast and resold in America for £40.

The approximate number of slaves which landed overseas between 1501 and 1888 was 9,475,000. This figure does not include those who died in raids, or in revolts inside the dungeons in the forts and in the terrible conditions of the slave ships at sea.

The slave trade resulted in loss of people and their labour, energy and skill. It also led to lack of peace and security as African slave traders seized people to sell to European slave traders. There was much suffering among communities such as the Igbo which lacked central government and thus fell easy prey to slave raids. A few African rulers and traders became rich from the slave trade, but Europe benefited most. In the Americas African slave labour cleared forests, developed plantations and mines and built cities, and thus helped the growth of white American prosperity.

Some African rulers such as King Agaja of Dahomey in 1724 and the *almami* of Futa Toro in 1789 tried to stop the slave trade, but they gave up their efforts when other rulers failed to support them.

Opposition to the slave trade and to slavery itself was carried out in the Americas as well as Africa. There were hundreds of small scale rebellions by slaves in the Americas. Two large scale rebellions succeeded in winning freedom for the slaves. The Maroons in the hills of Jamaica in the 18th century and the people of Haiti led by the great liberator, Toussaint L'Ouverture, in 1800 defeated British and French armies.

Key to map

→ African exports (slaves)
⇢ Other African exports:
    Gold
    Ivory
    Gum

→ Exports from the Americas:
    Tobacco
    Rum
    Sugar
    Cotton

⇢ European exports
    Manufactures:
    guns
    metalware
    cloth
    beads
    rum

▬ Portuguese colonies

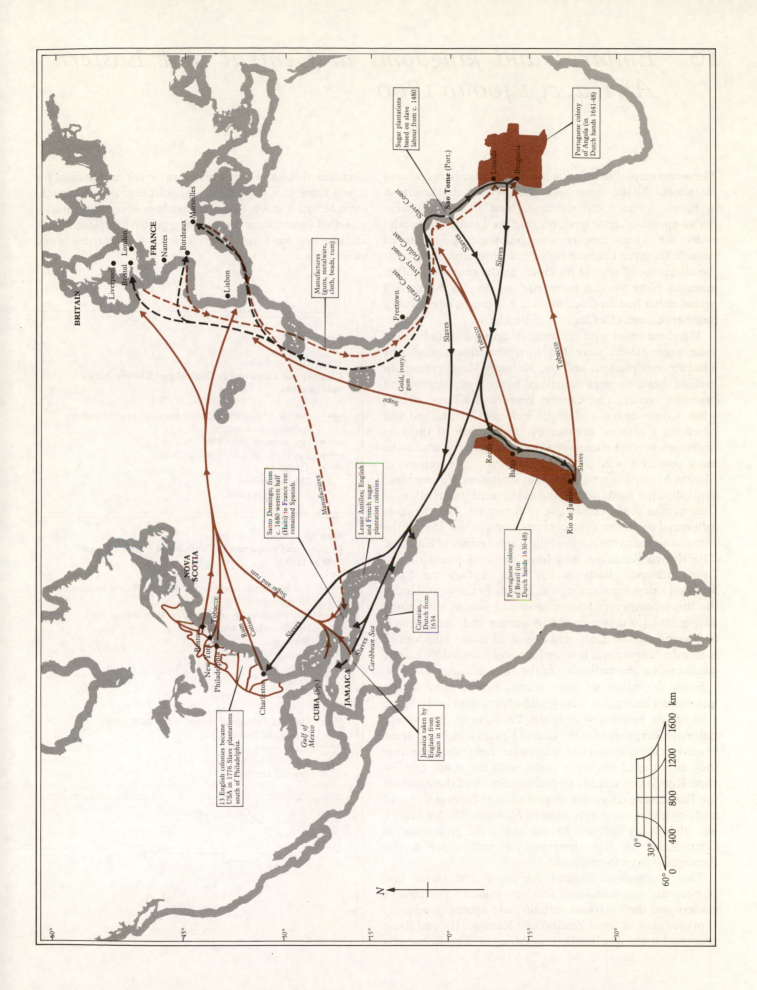

BRITAIN

Liverpool •
London •
Bristol •

FRANCE

Nantes •

Bordeaux •

Marseilles •

Lisbon •

Manufactures (guns, metalware, cloth, beads, rum)

Gold, ivory, gum

Freetown •

Grain Coast
Ivory Coast
Gold Coast
Slave Coast

Sugar

Sao Tome (Port.)

Slaves

Slaves

Luanda
Benguela

Sugar plantations based on slave labour from c. 1480

Portuguese colony of Angola (in Dutch hands 1641-48)

Tobacco

Tobacco

Recife
Bahia

Slaves

Rio de Janeiro

Slaves

Portuguese colony of Brazil (in Dutch hands 1630-48)

Manufactures

Santo Domingo; from c. 1680 western half (Haiti) to France rest remained Spanish.

Lesser Antilles; English and French sugar plantation colonies.

Curaçao, Dutch from 1634

NOVA SCOTIA

Boston •
New York •
Philadelphia •

Tobacco

Rum

Cotton

Sugar and rum

Charleston •

Slaves

Slaves

CUBA (Sp.)

Gulf of Mexico

JAMAICA

Caribbean Sea

Jamaica taken by England from Spain in 1665

13 English colonies became USA in 1776. Slave plantations south of Philadelphia.

N

0 400 800 1200 1600 km

0°
30°
60°

60°
45°
30°
15°
0°
15°
30°

These two maps illustrate the history of a number of powerful states. All of them were situated in the savannah or lightly forested environments, and all of them were Bantu-speaking (note however that the Luo invaders who ended the Kitara Empire were Nilotes). The territorial boundaries given here can only be an approximation, since the allegiance of distant provinces to the centre was often minimal. Note too that many African peoples during this period either had no chiefs at all (e.g. Tonga), or else had a number of small chiefdoms (e.g. Bemba).

The three zones with the longest continuous tradition of state organisation were the interlacustrine region, the Zimbabwean plateau, and the Katonga-Kasai region. In each of these, empires flourished in the 15th century and probably earlier. The Chwezi Empire of Kitara covered what is now central and south-western Uganda, and was based on a pastoral aristocracy. As a result of the Luo invasions, several successor states emerged, of which the most powerful was probably Bunyoro. The empire of Mwene Mutapa (a royal title, also written as *Monomotapa*) controlled the gold trade to the coast, until the rebellion of Changamire at the end of the 15th century. But the most influential of all the 15th century empires was that of the Luba, situated to the north of the copper mines of Katanga. The Kongo Kingdom may have owed its foundation to Luba influence. Early in the 17th century the Luba founded a new state among the Lunda to the west. Under the line of emperors known as *mwata yamvo*, the Lunda adapted the Luba system of government and then spread it to Kasanje, to the Lozi, and above all to the kingdom of Kazembe (also a royal title), which was founded by Lunda conquerors at the beginning of the 18th century.

From the 1480s all these states, except those in the interlacustrine region, were gradually brought into contact – direct or indirect – with the Portuguese. Portuguese influence was greatest in the case of Kongo which they tried to convert into a model Christian state; but at the same time they encouraged the slave trade, with the result that by 1600 Kongo was already in decline. South of the Zambezi the Portuguese (from the 1530s) tried to control the gold trade by giving support to Mwene Mutapa. But this empire was already in decline. In the 1690s the rival state of Changamire at last destroyed it and expelled the Portuguese from the plateau.

The Portuguese demand for ivory and slaves had important repercussions further inland. Portuguese traders and their African or half-caste agents (*pombeiros*) ventured only as far as Zumbo and Kasanje. Beyond those points all trade was handled by Africans. The Imbangala

kingdom of Kasanje acted as an important middleman, for it was there that the *pombeiros* could find goods brought from Mwata Yamvo. Along the trade-routes of the interior travelled firearms for the use of aggressive African rulers, and also new food crops from America (cassava, maize and sweet potato).

Key to maps

Map (A)
Empires and kingdoms in Central and Eastern Africa 1400 to 1600

— The boundaries marked show the empires and kingdoms at their greatest extent
--→ Jaga invasions from 1568
→ Luo invasions 15th-17th centuries
— Trade routes
▲ Mineral deposits
Tropical rain forest

Map (B)
Empires and kingdoms in Central and Eastern Africa 1600 to 1800

— The boundaries marked show the empires and kingdoms at their greatest extent
---- Boundaries of the interlacustrine kingdoms, c. 1800
Interlacustrine kingdoms
Bunyoro
Buganda
Nkore
Rwanda
Burundi

-- Limits of Portuguese control in the colonies of Angola and Mozambique
— Trade routes
▲ Mineral deposits
Tropical rain forest

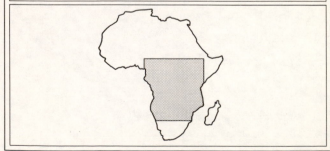

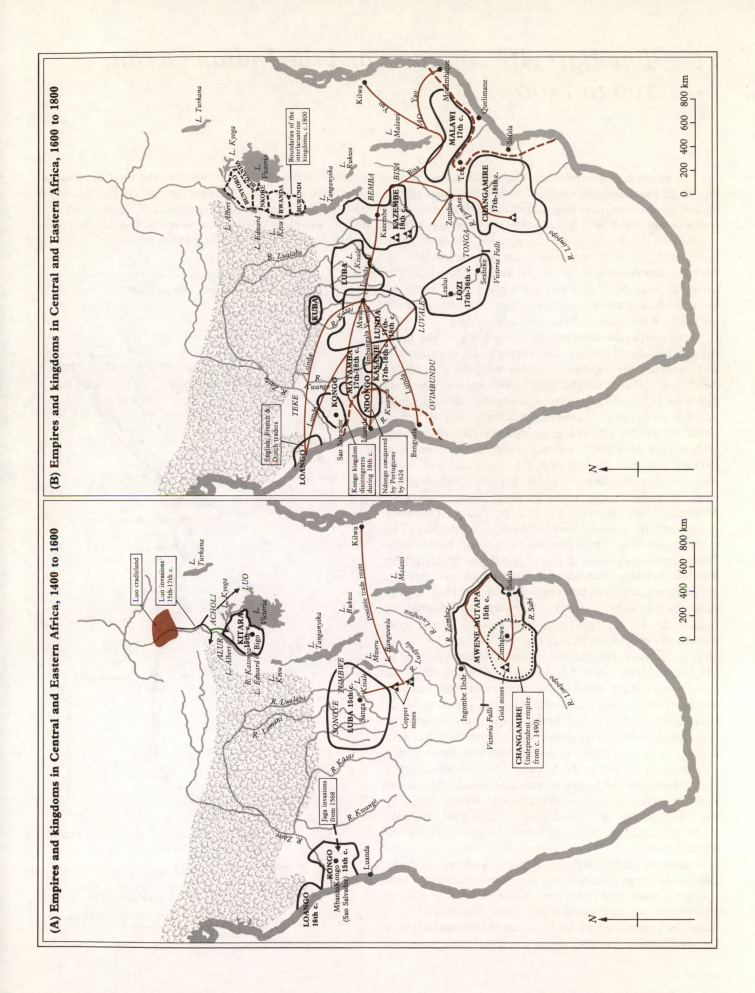

(B) Empires and kingdoms in Central and Eastern Africa, 1600 to 1800

0 200 400 600 800 km

N

Boundaries of the interlacustrine kingdoms, c.1800

English, French & Dutch traders

Kongo kingdom disintegrates during 18th c.

Ndongo conquered by Portuguese by 1624

KARAGWE
NKORE
RWANDA
BURUNDI
BUGANDA
L. Turkana
L. Kyoga
L. Victoria
L. Albert
L. Edward
L. Kivu
R. Lualaba
L. Tanganyika
L. Rukwa
L. Malawi
Kilwa
Mozambique
Quelimane
Sofala
MALAWI 17th c.
YAO
Yao
Yao
CHANGAMIRE 17th-18th c.
Zumbo
R. Zambezi
Tete
Bisa
BISA
BEMBA
Kazembe
KAZEMBE 18th c.
LUBA 17th-18th c.
L. Kisale
Mwata
Lunda
TONGA
LOZI 17th-18th c.
Lealui
Seskeke
Victoria Falls
LUVALE
KUBA
R. Kasai
Mwata Yamvo
imbangala
KASANJE LUNDA 17th-18th c.
MATAMBA 17th-18th c.
NDONGO
OVIMBUNDU
R. Kwango
Lunda
Lunda
Lunda
R. Kwanza
TEKE
KONGO
LOANGO
Sao Salvador
Luanda
Benguela
R. Zaire
R. Limpopo

(A) Empires and kingdoms in Central and Eastern Africa, 1400 to 1600

0 200 400 600 800 km

N

Luo cradleland

Luo invasions 15th-17th c.

Jaga invasions from 1568

CHANGAMIRE (independent empire from c. 1490)

L. Turkana
LUO
ACHOLI
ALUR
KITARA 16th c.
Bigo
L. Kyoga
L. Victoria
L. Albert
R. Katonga
L. Edward
L. Kivu
L. Tanganyika
R. Lualaba
R. Lomani
R. Kasai
R. Kwango
R. Zaire
SONGYE
LUBA 15th c.
Sanga
L. Kisale
TUMBWE 15th c.
Copper mines
L. Mweru
L. Bangweulu
R. Luapula
L. Rukwa
L. Malawi
possible trade route
Kilwa
Ingombe Ilede
Victoria Falls
R. Luangwa
R. Zambezi
MWENE-MUTAPA 15th c.
Zimbabwe
Sofala
Gold mines
R. Sabi
R. Limpopo
KONGO 15th c.
MbanzaKongo (Sao Salvador)
Luanda
LOANGO 16th c.

The East African coast and the Indian Ocean, 700 to 1500

For the entire coastline between Cape Guardafui and the mouth of the Zambezi, contacts with other parts of the Indian Ocean were more important during this period than contacts with the East African interior. This was partly on account of the inhospitable character of the immediate hinterland. But much more important was the fact that the East African coast was part of the Indian Ocean trading network. The coast received not only a wide range of imports but also an important addition to its population in the shape of immigrants from South-West Asia.

This commercial involvement dates back to the great days of the Roman Empire (1st century to 4th century A.D.) and probably earlier, but it is only with the rise of the Arabs and Islam that the picture becomes at all clear. From the 8th century the most active traders along the East African coast were Arabs from Oman and Arabised Persians from the Shiraz region. By the 11th century these traders had also made contact with Madagascar. The Persian Gulf in turn was linked by overland and ocean routes with both Europe and the Far East; this explains why, as early as the 10th century, Manda (north of Mombasa) was receiving Chinese porcelain. The main items brought to East Africa were cloth and pottery. The main exports from the region for most of this period were animal products (above all ivory) and slaves (though these were taken in large numbers only from the Horn of Africa). In the 10th century, however, gold from what is now Zimbabwe began to attract the traders as far south as Sofala, and by the 15th century, it was by far the most important export from East Africa.

The earliest permanent Arab settlements (e.g. Mogadishu, Brava, Manda) were founded in the 8th or 9th century from the Persian Gulf. Immigrants from this area and from South Arabia continued to trickle into East Africa right up until the 19th century. Expansion southwards from the Banadir Coast proceeded slowly until the late 12th century, when increased migration was associated with a ruling group known as the Shirazi. They colonised many places between the Lamu islands and Sofala. Much the most important of their settlements was Kilwa, which by the 14th century exercised sole control over the gold trade of Sofala (at the expense of Mogadishu's earlier ascendancy).

Successive groups of Arab immigrants merged with the Bantu-speaking Africans of the coast to produce in the 14th century a society of city-states whose religion was Islam and whose language was Swahili. Both religion and trade made the coastmen look to the ocean as their main line of communication. Except along the gold-trails near the

Zambezi, they did not journey into the interior; instead, ivory and skins were brought to the coastal towns by traders from the immediate hinterland. The coastmen were not to establish their own long-distance trade-routes overland until the 19th century (Map 20).

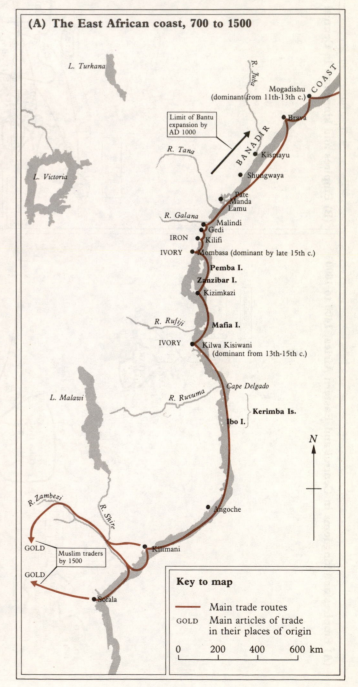

(A) The East African coast, 700 to 1500

L. Turkana

R. Juba

Mogadishu (dominant from 11th-13th c.)

Brava

Limit of Bantu expansion by AD 1000

BANADIR COAST

R. Tana

Kismayu

L. Victoria

Shungwaya

Pate
Manda
Lamu

R. Galana

Malindi
Gedi

IRON · Kilifi

IVORY · Mombasa (dominant by late 15th c.)

Pemba I.

Zanzibar I.

Kizimkazi

R. Rufiji

Mafia I.

IVORY · Kilwa Kisiwani (dominant from 13th-15th c.)

Cape Delgado

L. Malawi

R. Ruvuma

Kerimba Is.

Ibo I.

N

R. Zambezi

R. Shire

Angoche

GOLD

Muslim traders by 1500

Kilimani

GOLD

Sofala

Key to map

— Main trade routes

GOLD Main articles of trade in their places of origin

0   200   400   600 km

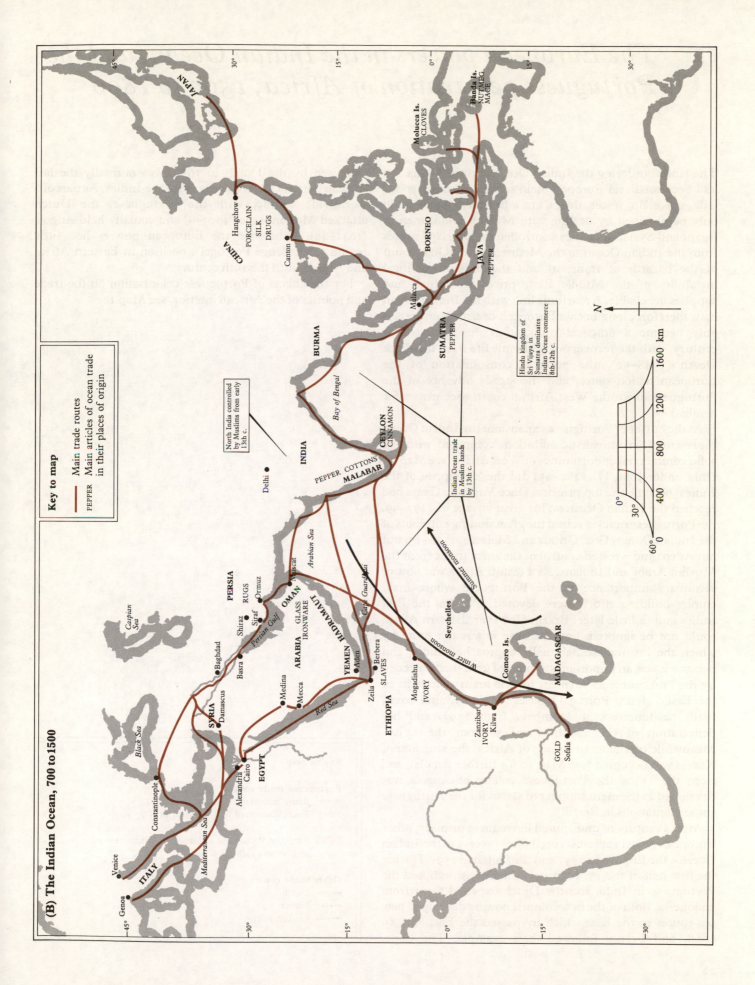

(B) The Indian Ocean, 700 to 1500

Key to map

— Main trade routes

— Main articles of ocean trade in their places of origin

PEPPER

North India controlled by Muslims from early 13th c.

Hindu kingdom of Sri Vijaya in Sumatra dominates Indian Ocean commerce 8th-12th c.

Indian Ocean trade in Muslim hands by 13th c.

JAPAN

CHINA
Hangchow PORCELAIN SILK DRUGS
Canton

BORNEO

JAVA PEPPER

SUMATRA PEPPER

Molucca Is. CLOVES

Banda Is. NUTMEG MACE

Malacca

BURMA

Bay of Bengal

INDIA
Delhi

MALABAR PEPPER COTTONS

CEYLON CINNAMON

Arabian Sea

Cape Guardafui

Summer monsoon

Winter monsoon

Seychelles

Comoro Is.

MADAGASCAR

PERSIA
RUGS
Ormuz
Siraf
Shiraz
Basra
Baghdad

Persian Gulf

OMAN Muscat

HADRAMAUT

ARABIA GLASS IRONWARE

YEMEN Aden Berbera

Zeila SLAVES

ETHIOPIA

Mogadishu IVORY

Zanzibar IVORY
Kilwa

Sofala GOLD

Caspian Sea

Black Sea

Constantinople

ITALY
Venice
Genoa

Mediterranean Sea

Alexandria Cairo **EGYPT**

SYRIA
Damascus
Medina
Mecca

Red Sea

0°   400   800   1200   1600 km

30°

60°

12 The European powers in the Indian Ocean, and the Portuguese penetration of Africa, 1500 to 1800

The lands bordering the Indian Ocean and the China Sea had been medieval Europe's main source of luxury goods (silk, porcelain, spices, drugs, etc.). But these goods could only be obtained by dealing with Muslim middlemen in Egypt and Syria, since they controlled the overland routes from the Indian Ocean to the Mediterranean. On account of the hazards of transport and the periodic political instability of the Middle East, prices were high and supplies unreliable. A maritime link with the Indian Ocean had, therefore, long been a European dream. However, it only became a practical proposition during the 15th century, with the recovery of economic life from the Black Death (1348–50), the political consolidation of the European nation-states, and the steady advance of the Portuguese down the West African coast. (See map 7 for details.)

At the outset of Portuguese expansion, the Indian Ocean represented an unrealistic ambition, compared with the solid commercial opportunities of West Africa (see Map 7). Only under John II (1481–95) did the 'enterprise of the Indies' become the top priority. Once Vasco da Gama had reached the Indian Ocean on his great voyage of 1497–99, the Portuguese quickly seized the great trading entrepots of the Indian Ocean (Goa, Ormuz and Malacca, 1510–15, but not Aden) and wrested control of the spice traffic from the Muslim Arabs and Indians. As a result, Africa was now of secondary importance to the Portuguese whose main empire-building efforts were devoted to India, the East Indies and (a little later) Brazil. However, Eastern Africa could not be ignored, both because it was the route by which the Portuguese habitually approached India, and because it was an important supplier of gold (badly needed by the Portuguese as payment for the luxury products of the East). Hence Portugal's bases on the Swahili coast, (with headquarters at Mombasa from 1593) and her penetration of the Zambezi valley from the 1530s. Meanwhile on the western side of Africa, the kingdom of Kongo was occupied (see Map 10 for further details), and from the 1570s the Portuguese colony of Angola was developed as the main supplier of slaves for the Portuguese sugar plantations in Brazil.

After a century of undisputed Portuguese primacy, other European powers at last secured direct access to the Indian Ocean – the English in 1591 and the Dutch in 1595. During the first half of the 17th century, the English eclipsed the Portuguese in India and the Dutch expelled them from Indonesia. Both of the new colonial powers developed new sea-routes to the East which by-passed the East African coast, and France followed their example. The Cape, colonised by the Dutch in 1652, was normally the last African port of call on the voyage to the Indies. As part of a worldwide conflict with the Portuguese, the Dutch attacked Mozambique (1607–8) and actually held Angola (1641–48). Otherwise the European powers had little reason to challenge Portugal's position in Eastern Africa and Angola until the 19th century.

For the effects of Portuguese colonisation on the trade and politics of the African interior, see Map 10.

Key to map

Portuguese trade routes
— Route discovered by Dias, 1487-8
– – Route discovered by Da Gama, 1497-9

▬ Extent of Portuguese influence in African interior in 17th and 18th centuries

Other trade routes
– – Dutch
······ French
—— English/British

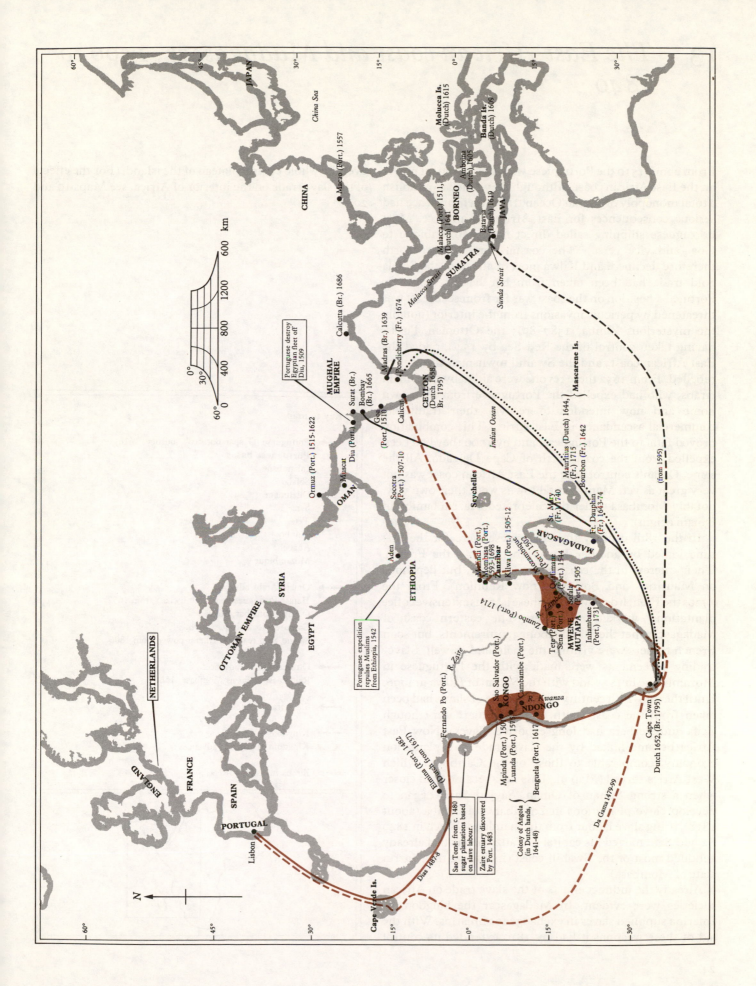

N

km
0   600   1200
0   400   800   1600

60°
30°
0°
30°
60°

ENGLAND
FRANCE
SPAIN
PORTUGAL
Lisbon

NETHERLANDS

OTTOMAN EMPIRE
SYRIA
EGYPT
ETHIOPIA

Aden

Ormuz (Port.) 1515-1622
Muscat
OMAN
Socotra (Port.) 1507-10
Diu (Port.)
Surat (Br.)
Bombay (Br.) 1665
Goa (Port.) 1510
Calicut

MUGHAL EMPIRE

Portuguese destroy
Egyptian fleet off
Diu, 1509

Portuguese expedition
repulses Muslims
from Ethiopia, 1542

CHINA
JAPAN

China Sea

Macao (Port.) 1557

Calcutta (Br.) 1686
Madras (Br.) 1639
Pondicherry (Fr.) 1674
CEYLON (Dutch 1658, Br. 1795)

Malacca (Port.) 1511, (Dutch) 1641
Malacca Strait
SUMATRA
Sunda Strait

BORNEO
Molucca Is. (Dutch) 1615
Banda Is. (Dutch) 1609
Amboina (Dutch) 1605
Batavia (Dutch) 1619
JAVA

Indian Ocean

Seychelles

Mascarene Is.
Mauritius (Dutch) 1644, (Fr.) 1715
Bourbon (Fr.) 1642

St. Mary (Fr.) 1740
MADAGASCAR
Ft. Dauphin (Fr.) 1643-74

from 1595

Melindi (Port.)
Mombasa (Port.) 1593-1698
Zanzibar
Kilwa (Port.) 1505-12

Mozambique (Port.) 1502
Zumbo (Port.) 1714
R. Zambezi
Quelimane (Port.) 1544
Sofala (Port.) 1505
Tete (Port.)
Sena (Port.)
MWENE MUTAPA
Inhambane (Port.) 1731

Cape Town
Dutch 1652, (Br. 1795)

Da Gama 1479-99

Fernando Po (Port.)
R. Zaire
Mpinda (Port.) 150
Sao Salvador (Port.)
KONGO
R. Kwanza
NDONGO
Luanda (Port.) 157
Cambambe (Port.) 1617
Benguela (Port.)

Colony of Angola
(in Dutch hands,
1641-48)

Elmina (Port.) 1482
(Dutch from 1637)

Sao Tomé: from c. 1480
sugar plantations based
on slave labour.

Zaire estuary discovered
by Port. 1483

Dias 1487-8

Cape Verde Is.
15°
0°
15°
30°

13 The East African coast and Madagascar, 1500 to 1840

From about 1510 the Portuguese were the dominant power on the East African coast. Although they failed to establish a total monopoly of Indian Ocean trade, their presence had serious consequences for East African commerce. Most Portuguese shipping sailed direct from Mozambique to Goa (and vice versa). The coastal ports further north therefore declined, and Kilwa most of all, since the Sofala gold trade had been taken from her hands. However, Portugal's position on the coast was far from secure. It was threatened by periodic invasions from the interior (notably the mysterious Zimba, 1587–89); the Ottoman Turks, having taken control of the Red Sea by 1540, raided the East African coast; and the Swahili townsmen themselves rebelled. From 1652 these revolts were aided by the Omani Arabs, who had expelled the Portuguese from their own home and now intended to recover their traditional commercial ascendancy in East Africa. This combination proved fatal to the Portuguese, and by 1700 they had been expelled from the coast north of Cape Delgado. All the same, Oman's control over the East African coast was not very great as yet. Many coastal towns went their own way, notably Mombasa under the celebrated Mazrui family (of Omani origin).

In the 18th century the Portuguese were for the first time joined by another European power – the French. Their interest in the coast was not direct, but depended on Mauritius and Bourbon (now Réunion). From the 1720s the French developed on these islands extensive coffee plantations, worked by slaves. The eastern coast of Madagascar met the initial labour requirements, but soon French traders were visiting the mainland as well. Slave-trading agreements were made with the Portuguese in Mozambique in 1735 and with the Sultan of Kilwa in 1776. Until the mid-18th century only a trickle of slaves had been taken from the coast south of Cape Guardafui (though Zeila and Berbera had long exported slaves). Now East Africa became linked by the slave trade to a plantation economy, comparable to those of the Caribbean which West Africa served (Map 9). This link became even closer when a strong Sultan of Oman, Sayyid Said, began to develop clove plantations in Zanzibar and Pemba (about 1818), using slave labour from the mainland. When in 1840 Sayyid Said moved his capital to Zanzibar, he had already subdued most of the Swahili coast (including the Mazrui state of Mombasa).

Already the indirect effects of the slave trade on African societies were evident. In Madagascar the kingdom of Imerina supplied slaves in exchange for firearms. With the aid of these weapons it had by 1810 extended its control over the whole central plateau of the island. (For the effects of the slave trade on the interior of Africa, see Maps 10 and 20).

Key to map

→ Portuguese (Gaspar Bocarro's journey, 1616)
Portuguese bases
Inhambane
Sofala
Quelimane
Sena
Tete
Zumbo
Angoche
Mozambique

→ Omani Arabs advance:
Harass Portuguese on Swahili coast from 1652;
Occupy Zanzibar, 1699;
Capture Mozambique, 1698;
Sayyid Said reasserts Omani power from 1806

→ Ottoman Turks advance:
Raid coast as far as Mombasa, 1586-8

→ Slave trade routes

—·— Kingdom of Imerina
↖ ↗ Kingdom of Imerina advances

····▶ Zimba invasion 1587-9

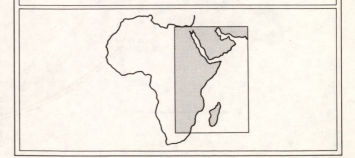

24

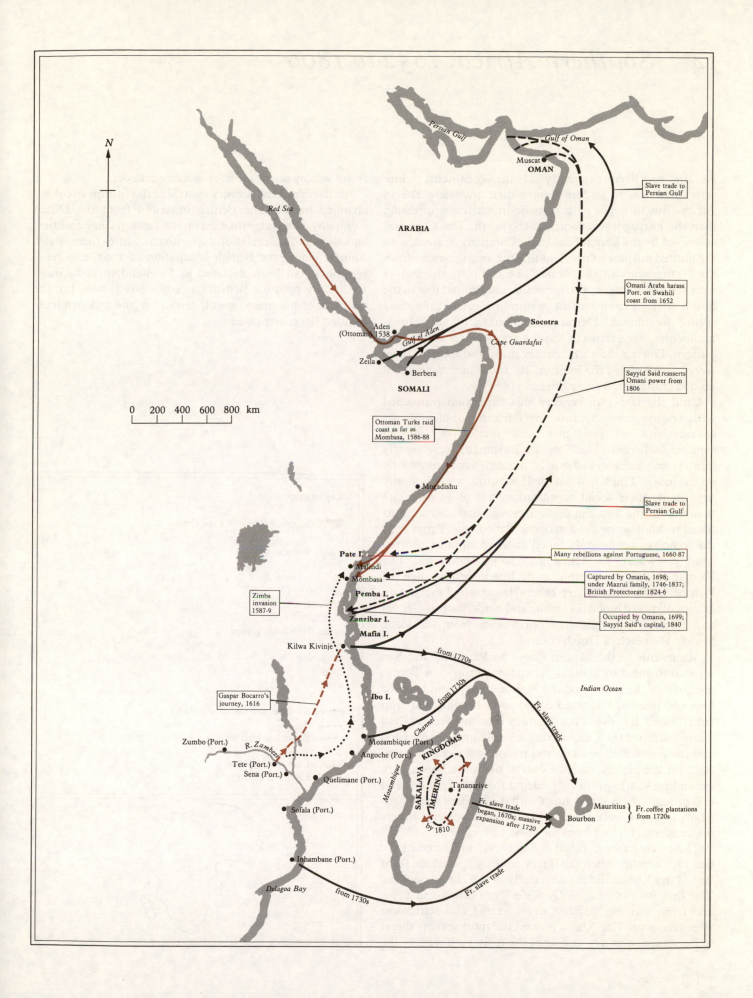

N

0 200 400 600 800 km

Red Sea

ARABIA

Persian Gulf

Gulf of Oman

Muscat

OMAN

Slave trade to
Persian Gulf

Omani Arabs harass
Port. on Swahili
coast from 1652

Aden
(Ottoman 1538)

Gulf of Aden

Zeila

Berbera

SOMALI

Socotra

Cape Guardafui

Sayyid Said reasserts
Omani power from
1806

Ottoman Turks raid
coast as far as
Mombasa, 1586-88

Mogadishu

Slave trade to
Persian Gulf

Pate I.

Malindi

Mombasa

Pemba I.

Many rebellions against Portuguese, 1660-87

Captured by Omanis, 1698;
under Mazrui family, 1746-1837;
British Protectorate 1824-6

Zimba
invasion
1587-9

Zanzibar I.

Mafia I.

Occupied by Omanis, 1699;
Sayyid Said's capital, 1840

Kilwa Kivinje

from 1770s

Gaspar Bocarro's
journey, 1616

Ibo I.

from 1730s

Mozambique
Channel

Indian Ocean

Fr. slave
trade

Zumbo (Port.)

R. Zambezi

Mozambique (Port.)

Tete (Port.)
Sena (Port.)

Angoche (Port.)

**SAKALAVA
KINGDOMS**

MERINA

Quelimane (Port.)

Tananarive

Fr. slave trade
began, 1670s; massive
expansion after 1720

Mauritius

Fr. coffee plantations
from 1720s

Sofala (Port.)

by 1810

Bourbon

Inhambane (Port.)

Delagoa Bay

from 1730s

Fr. slave trade

14   Southern Africa, 1652 to 1806

At the southern extremity of the continent, white settlement was to endure longer than anywhere else in Africa. But to begin with it made much less impression than the Portuguese colonies to the north. The Cape was colonised by the Dutch East India Company in 1652, with the limited purpose of provisioning the long sea-route from the Netherlands to Indonesia. The colonists themselves were soon thinking on a larger scale. They found that in the South African environment pastoralism offered the most secure livelihood. Despite the doubts of the Dutch authorities, open farms of about 2,500 hectares became the pattern. During the 18th century more and more of them were carved out of the interior. By 1800 there were about 10,000 Dutch farmers, or Boers.

Until the late 18th century this expansion proceeded with relative ease, because the African population was sparse, and its resistance was ineffective (though sometimes fierce). The San (or Bushmen) were mostly hunters and gatherers who lived in small bands constantly on the move. The Khoikhoi (or Hottentots) were basically herdsmen; their social organisation was more elaborate than that of the San, but neither group possessed an iron-based technology or lived in dense settlements. From 1716 the colonists increasingly relied on slave labour imported from elsewhere in Africa and from Indonesia. The Khoikhoi and San rapidly declined. Many died of European diseases. Many others became submerged in groups of mixed blood (i.e. white and black) such as Griqua and Korana, who migrated northwards from the Cape beyond the reach of Dutch control.

Meanwhile in the eastern Cape the Khoikhoi and San were confronted by another expanding group – the Bantu, comprising the Sotho and the Nguni. These peoples used iron and practised a mixed economy of herding and crop cultivation. By the 17th century Bantu-speakers had existed south of the Limpopo for several hundreds of years, and the population of the Natal region was already dense. Both on the plateau and the coastal plain the Bantu were expanding south-westwards during the 18th century, and this brought them into contact with the Khoikhoi and San. Many of these were absorbed into Bantu society; others migrated still further from the coast.

The circle of inter-racial contact was completed in the late 18th century when the Boers came up against the front line of the Xhosa, the most westerly of the Nguni peoples. The first Boer-Xhosa (or 'Kaffir') War occurred in 1779, and from then on disputes over grazing and settlement were frequent. The Xhosa proved the most serious threat to Boer expansion yet, and until the early 19th century the

result was by no means a foregone conclusion.

At the turn of the century control of the European colony changed hands. The British inherited from the Dutch Company a delicate situation on the eastern Cape frontier, and also a difficult relationship with the whites themselves. Shortly before the British occupation of 1795, two rebel republics had been declared at Swellendam and Graaff Reinet. By 1799 the British had suppressed these, but the problem of maintaining authority over the independent-minded Boers remained.

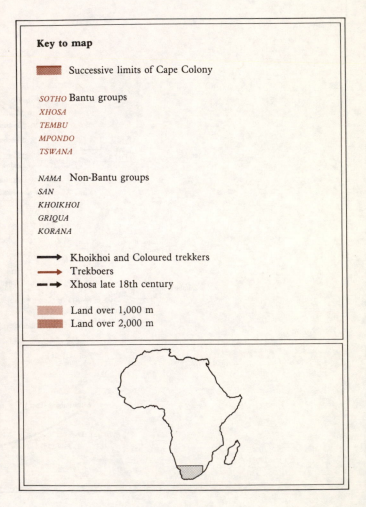

Key to map

▬ Successive limits of Cape Colony

SOTHO Bantu groups
XHOSA
TEMBU
MPONDO
TSWANA

NAMA Non-Bantu groups
SAN
KHOIKHOI
GRIQUA
KORANA

→ Khoikhoi and Coloured trekkers
→ Trekboers
--→ Xhosa late 18th century

▬ Land over 1,000 m
▬ Land over 2,000 m

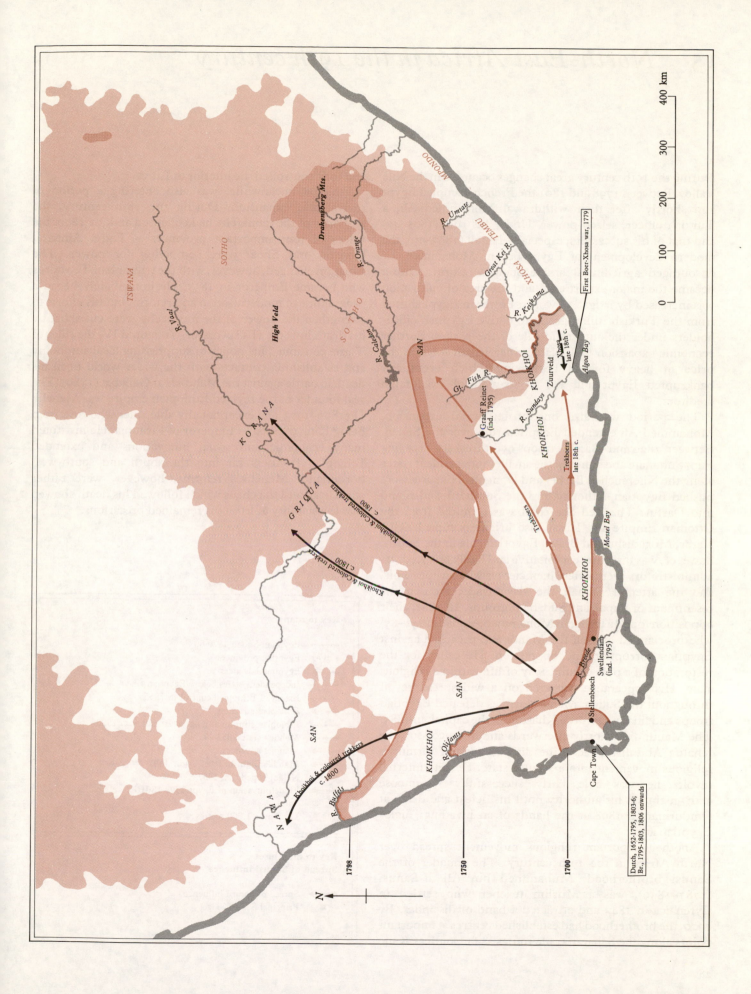

km
400
300
200
100
0

TSWANA

SOTHO

Drakensberg Mts.

High Veld

R. Vaal

R. Orange

R. Caledon

MPONDO

R. Umtata

TEMBU

Great Kei R.

XHOSA

R. Keiskama

SAN

Gt. Fish R.

Graaff Reinet
(ind. 1795)

R. Sundays

Zuurveld

Algoa Bay

KHOIKHOI

KHOIKHOI

Xhosa,
late 18th c.

First Boer-Xhosa war, 1779

KORANA

GRIQUA

Khoikhoi & Coloured trekkers
c. 1800

Khoikhoi & Coloured trekkers
c. 1800

Trekboers, late 18th c.

Trekboers

Trekboers, late 18th c.

Mossel Bay

KHOIKHOI

SAN

SAN

Khoikhoi & coloured trekkers
c. 1800

NAMA

R. Buffels

R. Olifants

KHOIKHOI

R. Breede

Stellenbosch

Swellendam
(ind. 1795)

Cape Town

Dutch, 1652-1795;
Br., 1795-1803, 1806 onwards

1798

1750

1700

N

During the 19th century great changes occurred in the Nile Valley. Between 1798 and 1801 the French occupied Egypt and shortly after their withdrawal Mohammed Ali, a Turkish officer, seized power. Under his rule (1805–49) and that of his successors, especially Ismail (1863–79), the modern development of Egypt began. Mohammed Ali encouraged agricultural and economic reform. Cotton became the major export crop and the area of cultivation was increased by irrigation works. Power in Egypt shifted from the Turkish ruling group to native Egyptian office-holders under the autocratic rule of the *pashas*. Further economic expansion took place under Ismail – but at the price of heavy foreign borrowing which eventually bankrupted Egypt and led to its control by foreign creditors.

The period was also one of territorial expansion. Mohammed Ali extended Egyptian rule over the Sudan. Between 1820 and 1822 his troops overthrew the decaying Funj Sultanate and annexed the smaller independent states along the Nile, such as Berber and Dongola. His successors pushed Egyptian authority into the Southern Sudan and into Darfur. The Red Sea coast was acquired from the Ottoman Empire and Ismail also briefly occupied Zeila, Harar, Mogadishu and Brava. Egyptian rule in the Sudan, however, was insecure, exploitative and badly financed. Its administrators were often inefficient and corrupt. This, and the attempt to halt the slave trade, aroused the resentment of important Sudanese groups. In 1881, their opposition found a leader in Mohammed Ahmad (1843–85) who proclaimed himself the Mahdi and preached against Egyptian corruption and oppression. He called for the restoration of a pure Islamic way of life within a religious state. His appearance triggered off a widespread revolt throughout the Sudan. Mahdist armies defeated Egyptian troops and finally captured Khartoum, the capital, in 1885. The Mahdi died shortly afterwards and his successor, the Khalifa Abdullahi, faced the difficult task of turning a religious movement into a secular state. Despite internal revolts he was able fairly successfully to impose and maintain his authority until his defeat and death at Omdurman in 1898 at the hands of an invading Anglo-Egyptian army.

Another important religious movement spread over North Africa in the 19th century. The founder of the Sanusi brotherhood, Muhammed bin Ali al-Sanusi (1787–1859), was a Muslim teacher who settled in Cyrenaica in 1843 and attracted a band of disciples. By 1900, the brotherhood had established centres at important points along the Saharan trade routes as far south as Kano and they controlled the interior of Libya.

Ethiopia, meanwhile, was also entering a period of revival and expansion. During the 18th century, the authority of the monarchy had collapsed and, by 1800, the rulers of four important provinces – Tigre, Amhara, Gojjam, and Shoa, were competing for power. The situation changed, however, with the triumph of Tewodros who became Emperor in 1855. He immediately began a programme of modernisation and reform, but his efforts to strengthen the power of the monarchy were cut short by his death in 1868. His successor, Yohannid IV, the ruler of Tigre, continued his policy of suppressing local autonomy and establishing contacts with the wider world until his death in battle against the Mahdists at Gallabat (1889). The real founder of the revived Ethiopian empire was Menelik II (1890–1913), an exceptionally able ruler who rose from being King of Shoa to Emperor of Ethiopia. He instituted many economic and social innovations and extended Ethiopian frontiers far into the south and south-west borderland. Menelik's reforms, however, were rather superficial and the chaos which followed his death showed that the stability of Ethiopia remained precarious.

Key to map

— Egyptian Sudan 1820-80
EGYPT Egyptian provinces
— → Egyptian advances
– – – Independent states before Egyptian rule
••••••• Extent of Ethiopian control to 1855
– –→ Ethiopian advances
— — Ethiopian Empire at its greatest extent c. 1900
—·— Mahdist state 1883-99
—·→ Mahdist advances
—·→ Mahdi's flight to Jebel Qadir 1881
⟹ Napier expedition 1867-8
⟹ French invasion of Egypt 1798-1801
▦ Sudd
▦ Land over 1,000 metres

Key to map inset
Spread of Sanusi influence

→ Spread of Sanusi influence
■ Principal Sanusi lodges

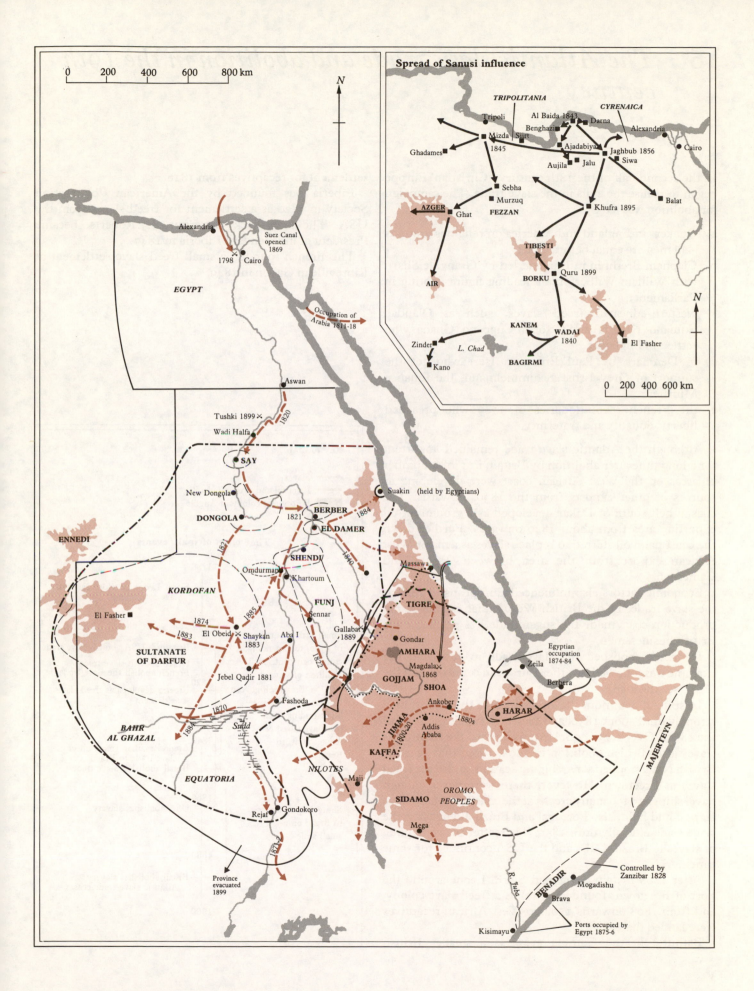

Spread of Sanusi influence

TRIPOLITANIA
CYRENAICA

Tripoli
Al Baida 1843
Darna
Alexandria
Mizda
Benghazi
Siirt
Cairo
Ghadames
1845
Ajadabiya
Jaghbub 1856
Aujila
Jalu
Siwa
Balat
Sebha
FEZZAN
Murzuq
Khufra 1895
AZGER
Ghat

TIBESTI

AIR
BORKU
Quru 1899

KANEM
WADAI
1840
El Fasher
Zinder
L. Chad
BAGIRMI
Kano

0   200   400   600 km

N

Alexandria
Suez Canal
opened
1869
1798   Cairo

EGYPT

Occupation of
Arabia 1811-18

Aswan

Tushki 1899 ×
Wadi Halfa
1820

SAY

New Dongola
Suakin   (held by Egyptians)
DONGOLA
1821   **BERBER**
1884
EL DAMER

SHENDI
Omdurman
Massawa
Khartoum
KORDOFAN
FUNJ
TIGRE
El Fasher
Sennar
SULTANATE
1874
El Obeid   Shaykan   Aba I   Gallabat
Gondar
Zeila
OF DARFUR
1883   1883   1889   **AMHARA**
Egyptian
occupation
1874-84
Jebel Qadir 1881
Magdala
1868
GOJJAM
Berbera
1870
SHOA
BAHR   1884   Fashoda   Ankober   1880s   **HARAR**
AL GHAZAL   *Sudd*
JIMMA
Addis
Ababa
EQUATORIA   *NILOTES*   Maji   1800-20
KAFFA
Rejaf   Gondokoro
SIDAMO   **OROMO**
Mega   **PEOPLES**
Province
evacuated
1899
1877

MAJERTEYN

R. Juba
Controlled by
Zanzibar 1828
BENADIR   Mogadishu
Brava
Kisimayu
Ports occupied by
Egypt 1875-6

0   200   400   600   800 km

N

16 *The Atlantic slave trade and abolition in the 19th century*

In the second half of the 18th century, 'Christian' Europe began to realise the evils in the slave trade. The campaign for abolition was led by:

a) Quakers in England and America on religious grounds – all men are equal before God;

b) Clapham Brethren in England led by Granville Sharp with William Wilberforce a leading figure fighting in Parliament;

c) western-educated freed slaves, such as Olaudah Equiano (Nigeria) and Ottobah Cugoano (Ghana) who settled in England;

d) in Denmark by Paul Erdmann Isert who got the support of Grev Ernst Schimmelmann, the Finance Minister;

e) the French revolutionaries of 1789 who preached liberty, equality and fraternity.

Although the Atlantic slave trade remained important for a long time after abolition by Britain in 1808 a number of areas on the West African coast were developing as sources of other exports from the 1830s onwards. The coastal belt south of Dakar developed as a groundnut oil exporting area from about 1840 onwards. Further down the coast palm oil started to replace slaves as a major West African export from the area between Asante and Cameroons.

Economic factors also influenced Europeans to abolish the slave trade. In the British West Indian islands rising production costs made the sugar trade less profitable for British businessmen.

Denmark abolished the slave trade in 1803 and her example was followed by other European countries and the USA (see the map).

In spite of abolition, the Atlantic slave trade continued strongly until about 1850, and then on a smaller scale until the 1880s. Over 1,750,000 Africans crossed the Atlantic as slaves after British abolition in 1808. From that year the British Navy stopped slave ships at sea and landed the freed slaves at Freetown. However, there were never enough naval ships and too many creeks at the coastline where slave ships could hide; also Portugal and Brazil did not stop the slave trade officially until 1850. Thereafter the smuggling of slaves to Brazil, Cuba and the USA continued for some time.

After 1808 Britain developed Sierra Leone around the port of Freetown (founded 1787) as a freed slave colony, and from 1808 onwards 150,000 West African recaptives were landed there.

Bathurst in the Gambia grew as a smaller British settlement for recaptives from 1816.

Liberia was founded by the American Colonisation Society in 1820 as a settlement for freed slaves from the USA. The first black Governor, J.J.Roberts, became President of independent Liberia in 1847.

The French founded a small freed slave settlement at Libreville in Gabon in 1849.

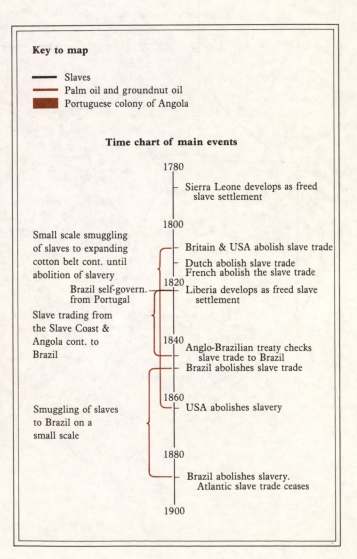

Key to map

— Slaves
— Palm oil and groundnut oil
■ Portuguese colony of Angola

Time chart of main events

1780
— Sierra Leone develops as freed slave settlement

1800

Small scale smuggling of slaves to expanding cotton belt cont. until abolition of slavery
— Britain & USA abolish slave trade
— Dutch abolish slave trade
French abolish the slave trade

1820
Brazil self-govern. from Portugal
— Liberia develops as freed slave settlement

Slave trading from the Slave Coast & Angola cont. to Brazil

1840
— Anglo-Brazilian treaty checks slave trade to Brazil
— Brazil abolishes slave trade

1860
Smuggling of slaves to Brazil on a small scale
— USA abolishes slavery

1880
— Brazil abolishes slavery. Atlantic slave trade ceases

1900

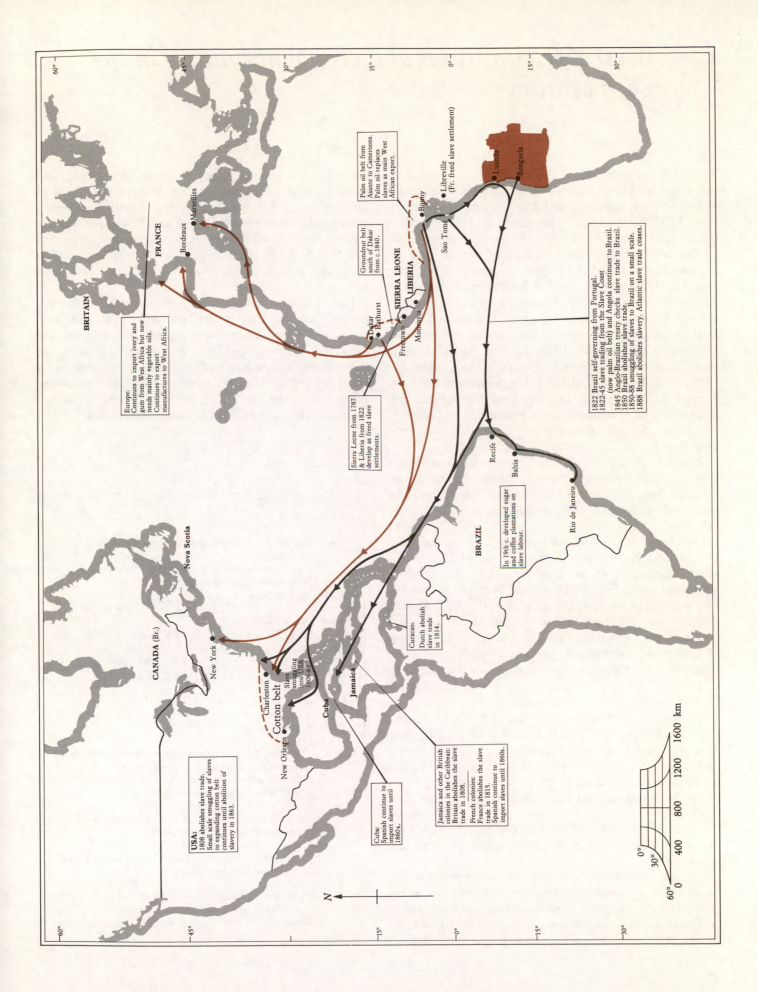

Palm oil belt from
Asante to Cameroons.
Palm oil replaces
slaves as main West
African export.

Groundnut belt
south of Dakar
from c.1840.

SIERRA LEONE
LIBERIA

Librecille (Fr. freed slave settlement)
Bopny
Sao Tomé
Luanda
Benguela

Dakar
Bathurst
Freetown
Monrovia

BRITAIN

FRANCE
Marseilles
Bordeaux

Europe:
Continues to import ivory and
gum from West Africa but now
needs mainly vegetable oils.
Continues to export
manufactures to West Africa.

1822 Brazil self-governing from Portugal.
1822-45 slave trading from the Slave Coast
(now palm oil belt) and Angola continues to Brazil.
1845 Anglo-Brazilian treaty checks slave trade to Brazil.
1850 Brazil abolishes slave trade.
1850-88 smuggling of slaves to Brazil on a small scale.
1888 Brazil abolishes slavery. Atlantic slave trade ceases.

Sierra Leone from 1787
& Liberia from 1822
develop as freed slave
settlements.

Recife
Bahia
Rio de Janeiro

BRAZIL

In 19th c. developed sugar
and coffee plantations on
slave labour.

Nova Scotia

CANADA (Br.)

New York

Curaçao:
Dutch abolish
slave trade
in 1814.

Charleston
Cotton belt
New Orleans
Slave
smuggling
into USA
1808-65

Cuba
Jamaica

USA:
1808 abolishes slave trade.
Small scale smuggling of slaves
to expanding cotton belt
continues until abolition of
slavery in 1863.

Cuba:
Spanish continue to
import slaves until
1860s.

Jamaica and other British
colonies in the Caribbean:
Britain abolishes the slave
trade in 1808.
French colonies:
France abolishes the slave
trade in 1815.
Spanish continue to
import slaves until 1860s.

N

0   400   800   1200 1600 km

17 *West African states and economic change in the 19th century*

The Islamic revolutions of the 19th century changed the political map of West Africa. Uthman dan Fodio, a Muslim Fulani scholar, led a successful revolt against the Hausa ruler of Gobir in 1804. The whole of Hausaland was conquered (1804–10) by his flag bearers who became emirs (rulers) of the Hausa states which now became part of a Fulani empire, called the Sokoto Caliphate. Inspired by events in Hausaland, Ahmad Lobbo, another Fulani, set up a reformed Muslim state in Macina on the upper Niger. In Kanem-Borno, al-Kanemi reformed Islam along Fulani lines, defended Borno against Fulani attack, and expanded his country's boundaries. In the far west, Al Hajj Umar, a Tokolor, also influenced by Sokoto, created a great Islamic empire from Futa Jalon to Timbuktu. South of the Tokolor Empire of Umar was the Mandinka Empire of the great gold and cattle trader, Samori Toure, created between 1870–85. To the east of Samori was the expanding Dyula commercial empire of Kong.

Asante expanded in all directions under Osei Bonsu, (1821–24) but from 1826 Asante steadily declined under pressure from Britain at the Gold Coast, where the Fante organised themselves into a short-lived Confederation (1868–71).

Dahomey expanded into the western slave coast states of Ouidah and Porto Novo at the expense of Oyo, which under Fulani pressure broke up after 1817. Ilorin became an emirate under Sokoto. The rest of Yorubaland broke up into warring city-states; the most powerful were Ibadan, which came to dominate most of Yorubaland (1860–93), and the Egba Confederacy around Abeokuta. The wars in Dahomey and Yorubaland were fought to control the new palm oil trade, which also came to dominate the economies of Benin, the Niger Delta city states from Ebrohimi to Opobo, Calabar, and the Igbo communities.

European imperialism also changed West Africa's political map, as the French expanded in Senegal from 1854 to control the new groundnut trade, and Britain extended her control in Sierra Leone and the Gambia (freed slave settlements), at the Gold Coast in 1873 (trade rivalry with Asante) and Lagos in 1861 (to stop the slave trade).

Liberia developed as an independent state after 1847 and became a major exporter of coffee, sugar, palm oil and camwood.

The economy of West Africa in the 19th century became much more dependent on trade with Europeans at the coast. The main imports were metal goods, textiles, spirits (gin and rum) and salt. Samori developed a new trade route to Freetown in order to buy guns there. West Africa's exports were mainly palm oil (from the 1830s) and groundnut oil (from the 1850s) to serve the needs of industrialising Europe and North America. Asante's coastal gold trade remained important. So did the Atlantic slave trade for a long time after abolition by Britain in 1808 (see Map 16). The trans-Saharan trade became much less important though it did not seriously decline until after 1875.

Internal trade was dominated by items such as kola nuts, horses, cattle, cotton cloth, foodstuffs, salt, local iron goods, and slaves. The most prominent African traders in the grasslands were the Dyula who operated between the upper Niger and Asante and the Hausa who traded as far afield as Yorubaland and Asante in the West and Borno and Adamawa in the east. The cities of Jenne, Kano and Kumasi were the main hubs of major trade routes.

Key to map

- Tropical rain forest boundary (between grasslands and forest)
- Desert boundary (between desert and grasslands)
- Areas occupied by colonial powers
- Main trade routes

Main items of trade:

C	Cattle, and hides and skins	**Gu**	Gum
Cc	Cotton cloth	**I**	Indigo
Cd	Camwood	**P**	Palm products
Ce	Coffee	**S**	Sugar
G	Gold		
Gn	Groundnuts		

Guide to the key:

1 *Kola nuts*
These were the main item of trade northwards from the coastal forest and the southern grasslands. Their production and trade was so widespread that they cannot be marked on the map in particular places.

2 *Horses*
The horse trade was universal in the grasslands and cannot be marked in particular places.

3 *Cattle and cotton cloth*
Trade in these items was widespread. Only the main areas of production have been shown.

4 *Other items*
Production and trading of *foodstuffs, salt* and local *iron goods* and trading of *ivory* and slaves was so widespread that they cannot be marked in particular places

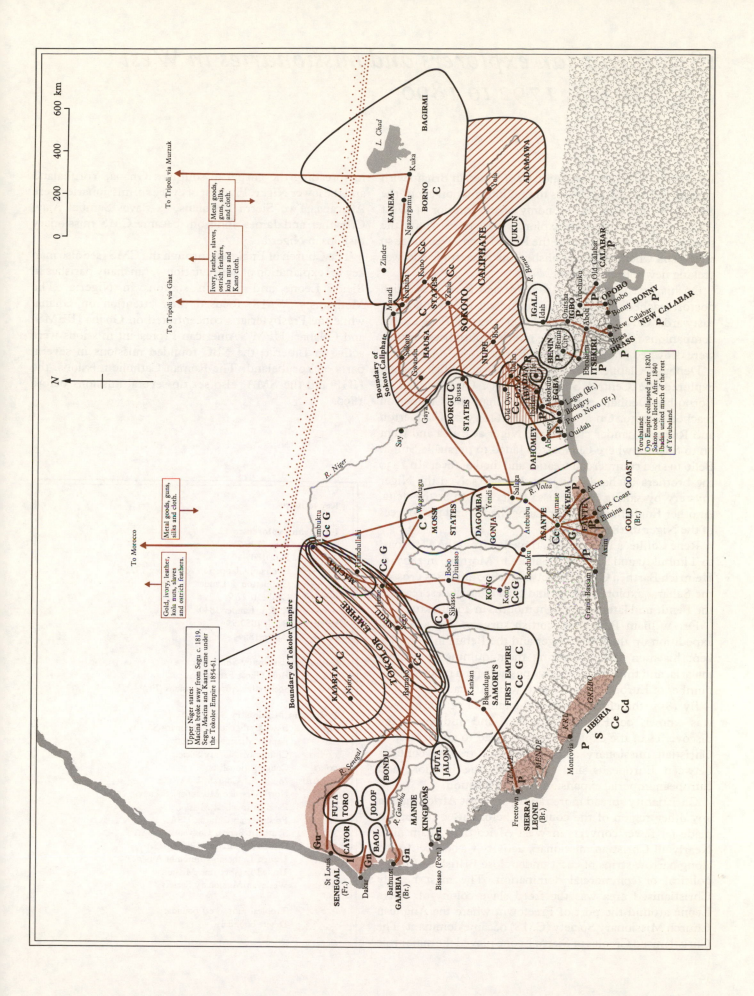

600 km
600 400 200 0

To Tripoli via Murzuk

Metal goods,
guns, silks,
and cloth.

Ivory, leather, slaves,
ostrich feathers,
kola nuts and
Kano cloth.

To Tripoli via Ghat

N

Boundary of Sokoto Caliphate

To Morocco

Metal goods, guns,
silks and cloth.

Gold, ivory, leather,
kola nuts, slaves
and ostrich feathers.

Boundary of Tokolor Empire

Upper Niger states:
Macina broke away from Segu c. 1819.
Segu, Macina and Kaarta came under
the Tokolor Empire 1854–61.

Yorubaland:
Oyo Empire collapsed after 1820.
Sokoto took Ilorin. After 1840
Ibadan united much of the rest
of Yorubaland.

L. Chad

BAGIRMI

Kuka

KANEM-
BORNO C

Ngazargamu
Zinder

Maradi
Katsiba   Kano Cc
Gaya   Zaria Cc

HAUSA
STATES C
Sokoto
Gwandu

SOKOTO
CALIPHATE

ADAMAWA
Yola

R. Benue

JUKUN

IGALA
Idah

NUPE
Bida
Bussa

BORGU C
STATES
Bussa

Say

R. Niger

Timbuktu
Cc G

Hamdullahi
Cc G

MACINA C

SEGU EMPIRE
Segu
Sansanding

TOKOLOR EMPIRE C

KAARTA C
Nioro

Bamako
Cc

Bakel

Kankan

Bhandugu
SAMORI'S
FIRST EMPIRE
Cc G C

FUTA
JALON

R. Senegal

BONDU

FUTA
TORO
CAYOR
BAOL
JOLOF

MANDE
KINGDOMS
Gn

R. Gambia

St Louis
SENEGAL
(Fr.)
Dakar
Gn

Bathurst
GAMBIA
(Br.)
Gn

Bissao (Port.)

Say

Wagadugu
C
MOSSI
STATES

DAGOMBA Yendi
GONJA
Salaga
Atebubu

Bobo
Diulasso

Sikasso C

KONG
Kong
Cc G

Bonduku

R. Volta

ASANTE
Cc
Kumase

AKYEM P
Accra

FANTE P
Cape Coast
Elmina

GOLD COAST
(Br.)
Axim P

Grand Bassam

TEMBU
MENDE
KRU
GREBO

Freetown
SIERRA
LEONE
(Br.)

Monrovia
LIBERIA
S   Ce Cd
P

Old Oyo
Oyo Cc
Ife
IJEBU
Ibadan
Abeokuta
EGBA P
Ilorin

DAHOMEY
Abomey
Porto Novo (Fr.)
Ouidah
Badagry
Lagos (Br.)

BENIN
Benin
City P

Ebrohimi
ITSEKIRI P

Onitsha
IGBO
Aboh
Brass
BRASS P

IGALA
Idah

Arochuku
Bonny

OPOBO
Opobo
Old Calabar
CALABAR P
New Calabar
NEW CALABAR P
BONNY P

18 European explorers and missionaries in West Africa, 1792 to 1890

In 1788 the African Association was formed in Britain with the aim of sending explorers to find information about the geography, politics and economy of the interior of West Africa. In particular these explorers were to search for the source, course and mouth of the River Niger, even more so after 1808 when Britain abolished the slave trade and was seeking new sources of trade.

On his first journey (1795–7) Mungo Park, a Scottish doctor, reached the Niger at Segu and saw the river flowing eastwards. On his second expedition (1805–6) Park and his companions failed to reach the river's mouth because they were drowned in the rapids near Bussa.

Denham, Clapperton and Oudney, three British officers, explored the Central Sudan (1822–5). Oudney died in Borno but Denham explored Lake Chad and Clapperton reached Sokoto. On a later journey (1825–7) Clapperton and Richard Lander crossed the Niger at Bussa and went on to Sokoto, where Clapperton failed to persuade Sultan Bello to sign commercial treaties and died of fever. In 1830 the brothers Richard and John Lander solved the Niger mystery by sailing from Bussa to its mouth at the delta. Another Englishman, Major Laing, had found the sources of the Niger in 1822.

Réné Caillié, a Frenchman, travelled from the west coast to Timbuktu and across the Sahara to Morocco in 1827–9. Heinrich Barth, a German, between 1850 and 1855 crossed the Sahara, explored Borno and the Hausa states, reached the Benue and later spent eight months in Timbuktu.

Dr. William Baikie, a Scottish surgeon, led a British expedition up the lower Niger and the Benue in 1854. He kept his men alive by giving them quinine to combat malaria, and thus showed it was possible for a much greater number of Europeans to come to West Africa.

By 1855, therefore, much of the interior of West Africa was known to Europe. Directly and indirectly the discoveries of the explorers were to lead to an increase in Christian missionary activities; active trading contacts between Europeans and peoples in the interior; and European imperial expansion and colonisation.

Christianity spread more rapidly in West Africa than in any other region of the continent before 1890 (though it made far fewer converts in West Africa than Islam did). Nearly all Christian missionary activity was concentrated along narrow strips of coast under close British or French political or commercial domination. The most heavily Christianised area was the freed slave colony of Sierra Leone around the port of Freetown, where the Anglican Church Missionary Society (CMS) became dominant. The Christianised Creoles of Sierra Leone played the major role

in spreading the gospel to southern Ghana, Yorubaland and the lower Niger. Five out of every six missionaries were Africans. Two Sierra Leonians, ex-slaves Samuel Ajayi Crowther and James Johnson, became CMS missionary bishops in Nigeria.

The Church of England, through the CMS (see also map key for explanation of abbreviations), ran many parishes in Sierra Leone and mission stations in Nigeria. The Methodists (WMS) focused their attention on Ghana, while the Presbyterians concentrated on Ghana (BEMS) and Calabar (UPM). American Protestant missions were active in Liberia; the SBC founded missions in several parts of Yorubaland. The Roman Catholic missions, the HGF and the SMA, also set up several missions before 1890.

Key to map

European explorers:
- – – –   Park 1795-7
- ———   Park 1805-6
- – – –   Denham, Clapperton & Oudney 1822-5
- – – – –   Clapperton & Lander 1825-7
- – – – –   Caillié 1827-9
- ·········   R. & J. Lander 1830
- ———   Barth 1850-55
- ·········   Baikie 1854

Catholic Missionary Societies:

HGF	Holy Ghost Fathers
SMA	Society for African Missions (Fr.)

Protestant Missionary Societies:

BEMS	Basel Evangelical Missionary Society
BMS	Baptist Missionary Society
CMS	Church Missionary Society
CONG	Congregationalists
METH (US)	Methodist Church, USA
NGMS	North German Missionary Society
PEM	Paris Evangelical Mission
PRES (US)	Presbyterian Church, USA
SBC	Southern Baptist Convention, USA
UBC	United Brethren in Christ, USA
ULCA	United Lutheran Church of America
UPM	United Presbyterian Mission
WMS	Wesleyan Missionary Society

Tropical rain forest boundary
Desert boundary

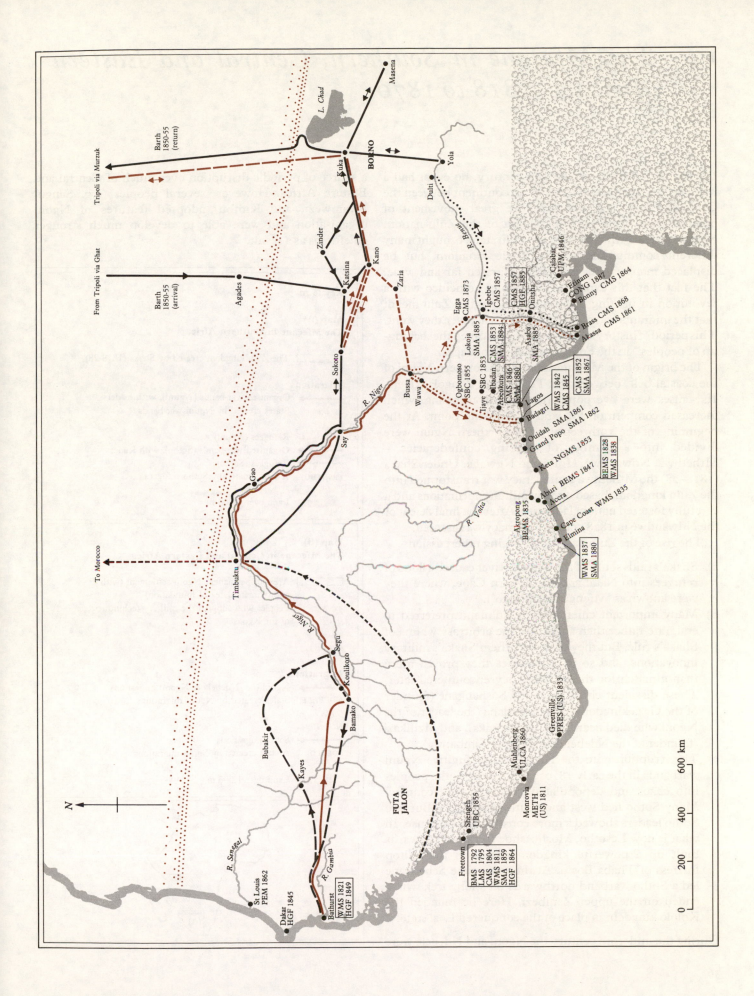

Masena

L. Chad

Barth 1850-55 (return)

Tripoli via Murzuk

From Tripoli via Ghat

Barth 1850-55 (arrival)

Kuka

BORNO

Zinder

Kano

Katsina

Zaria

Agades

Yola

Dulti

R. Benue

Calabar UPM 1846

Etinam

CONG 1887

Bonny CMS 1864

Onitsha

Asaba SMA 1885

CMS 1857 HGF 1885

Brass CMS 1868

Akassa CMS 1861

Egga CMS 1873

Igbebe CMS 1857

Lokoja SMA 1865

CMS 1853 SMA 1884

Ogbomoso SBC 1855

SBC 1853

Ibadan CMS 1846 SMA 1880

Abeokuta

Ijaye

Lagos WMS 1842 CMS 1845

CMS 1852 SMA 1867

Badagri

Ouidah SMA 1861

Grand Popo SMA 1862

Keta NGMS 1853

Aburi BEMS 1847

BEMS 1828 WMS 1838

Accra

Akropong BEMS 1835

Cape Coast WMS 1835

Elmina WMS 1837 SMA 1880

R. Volta

Sokoto

Say

Gao

Bussa

Wawa

R. Niger

To Morocco

Timbuktu

Segu

Koulikoro

Bamako

Bubakir

Kayes

FUTA JALON

R. Niger

R. Senegal

R. Gambia

St Louis PEM 1862

Dakar HGF 1845

Bathurst WMS 1821 HGF 1849

Shengh UBC 1855

Freetown BMS 1792 LMS 1795 CMS 1804 WMS 1811 SMA 1859 HGF 1864

Monrovia METH (US) 1811

Muhlenberg ULCA 1860

Greenville PRES (US) 1833

N

600 km

400

200

0

19 The Mfecane in Southern, Central and Eastern Africa, c. 1818 to 1870

During the first half of the 19th century, no event had a more profound effect on the African continent between the Cape and Lake Victoria than the great movement of peoples set in train by the creation of the Zulu nation. Shaka, the ruler who founded the Zulu state, brought many different communities into a single kingdom, but he displaced many more, and these migrated far and wide. The fact that this explosion of peoples coincided with a revolution in fighting techniques among the Zulu meant that the migrants had a violent impact wherever they went. This period of history is known as the Mfecane ('the shaking-up of peoples') in the Southern Bantu languages.

The origin of the Mfecane among the northern Nguni of the coastal belt, between the Tugela and Pongola Rivers. Its causes were overpopulation and overgrazing which increased competition for land to breaking point. At the beginning of the 19th century the northern Nguni were divided into a number of warring confederacies – Mthethwa, Ndwandwe, Hlubi and Ngwane. Under Shaka (1818–28) the Mthethwa confederacy was transformed into the Zulu kingdom, based on new military formations and a carefully fostered national identity. After the final defeat of the Ndwandwe in 1828, Zulu supremacy was assured.

The rise of the Zulu had wide-ranging repercussions:

a) Shaka's raids south of the Tugela River caused a flood of refugees into Natal and the eastern Cape, where they were known as 'Mfengu' (or 'Fingo').

b) Many important chiefs within Zululand preferred to emigrate rather than submit to the arbitrary whims of Shaka's rule. But they took with them Shaka's military innovations, and so in most cases they proved more than a match for the peoples they encountered later. These dissident chiefs included Soshangane (founder of the Gaza kingdom), Zwangendaba (the leader of the Ngoni who died near Lake Tanganyika), and Mzilikazi (founder of the Ndebele kingdom in Zimbabwe).

c) The irruption onto the High Veld of fugitive Nguni warbands in the early 1820s plunged the Sotho peoples into chaos and depopulated great tracts of country. Many Sotho fled west and south as refugees. But two Sotho leaders showed a more constructive response. In what is now Lesotho, Moshoeshoe from 1827 onwards built up a powerful kingdom based on the hilltop fortress of Thaba Bosiu. At the same time Sebetwane led a Sotho warband northwards on a long trek which ended on the upper Zambezi. Here he founded the Kololo kingdom in place of the conquered Lozi state.

During the mid-19th century the Ngoni and Ndebele were a source of periodic disruption over much of Central and Eastern Africa. However, several peoples (e.g. Sangu, Nyamwezi, and Kimbu) adopted features of Ngoni organisation and were able to develop much stronger chiefdoms as a result.

Key to maps

Map (A)
The Mfecane in Southern Africa

[⎯⎯⎯] The Zulu kingdom created by Shaka (1818-28)

Migrations

→ Organised war-bands (Nguni), with leaders
SWAZI States created by Nguni war-bands
GAZA

--→ Refugees (Nguni)
→ Organised war-bands (Sotho), with leaders
--→ Refugees (Sotho)
LESOTHO A state created by Sotho refugees

▨ Land over 1,000 m

Map (B)
The Mfecane in Central and Eastern Africa

[⎯⎯⎯] Areas of permanent Ngoni settlement (with approximate dates of foundation)
SANGU Peoples who adopted the military techniques
HEHE of the Ngoni
KIMBU
NYAMWEZI

Migrations

→ Nguni (i.e. Ndebele & Ngoni) migrations
NDEBELE States created by Nguni migrations
GAZA
NGONI

→ Sotho migrations
KOLOLO A state created by Sotho migrations

▨ Land over 1,000 m

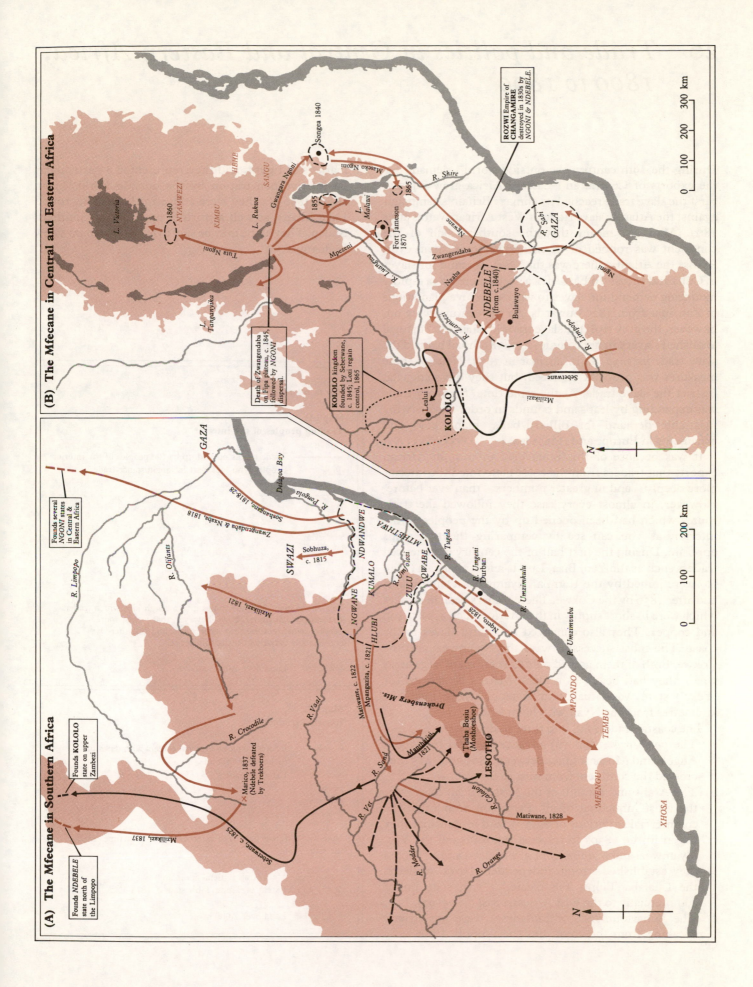

(A) The Mfecane in Southern Africa

Founds NDEBELE state north of the Limpopo

Founds KOLOLO state on upper Zambezi

Founds several NGONI states in Central & Eastern Africa

R. Limpopo

R. Olifants

GAZA

SWAZI

Delagoa Bay

R. Pongola

Sobhuza, c. 1815

Zwangendaba & Nxaba, 1818

Soshangane, 1818-28

Mzilikazi, 1821

NGWANE

NDWANDWE

KUMALO

HLUBI

MTHETHWA

ZULU

QWABE

R. Umgolozi

R. Tugela

R. Umgeni Durban

R. Umzimkulu

Ndeto, 1828

R. Crocodile

×Marico, 1837 (Ndebele defeated by Trekboers)

Sebetwane, c. 1835

R. Vaal

Mzilikazi, 1837

Matiwane, c. 1822

Mpangazita, c. 1821

Mantatisi, 1821

R. Sand

R. Vet

R. Modder

Drakensberg Mts.

•Thaba Bosiu (Moshoeshoe)

LESOTHO

R. Caledon

R. Orange

Matiwane, 1828

MPONDO

TEMBU

'MFENGU'

XHOSA

R. Umzimvubu

N

0   100   200 km

(B) The Mfecane in Central and Eastern Africa

ROZWI Empire of CHANGAMIRE destroyed in 1830s by NGONI & NDEBELE.

L. Victoria

NYAMWEZI 1860

HEHE

KIMBU

SANGU

Gwangara Ngoni

L. Rukwa

•Songea 1840

Maseko Ngoni

1855

1865

R. Shire

L. Malawi

Fort Jameson 1870

Mpezeni

R. Luangwa

Tuta Ngoni

L. Tanganyika

Death of Zwangendaba on Fipa plateau, c. 1845, followed by NGONI dispersal.

KOLOLO kingdom founded by Sebetwane, c. 1845; Lozi regain control, 1865

•Lealui

KOLOLO

Sebetwane

Mzilikazi

R. Zambezi

Nsane

Zwangendaba

Nxaba

NDEBELE (from c. 1840)

•Bulawayo

GAZA

R. Sabi

Ngoni

R. Limpopo

N

0   100   200   300 km

20 Trade and politics in Central and Eastern Africa, 1800 to 1890

During the 19th century the outside world's demand for the exports of Central and Eastern Africa grew rapidly. First the slave trade reached its climax: Britain's campaign against the Atlantic slave trade in West African waters after 1807 (Map 16) meant that the southern half of the continent was robbed of its manpower more than ever. Across the Atlantic there was the heavy demand for slaves in Cuba and Brazil. In East Africa itself, there was a rapidly mounting demand for slaves to work the clove plantations of Zanzibar from 1820 onwards. As the century wore on, however, the growth of the slave trade levelled off. Portugal abolished slavery in her colonies in 1838; Brazil banned the slave trade in 1850, and Zanzibar in 1873. None of these measures was properly enforced, but they did somewhat restrict the slave trade. At the same time, the ivory trade was expanding by leaps and bounds in order to satisfy the insatiable demand for billiard-balls, piano keys and ornaments in Europe and America.

It was because of this intensified interest in African exports that traders from the coast penetrated the interior more deeply – and in greater numbers – than ever before. However, in almost every case they followed the trade routes which had been opened up by the peoples of the interior, as you can see by comparing the two maps opposite. During the first half of the century experienced traders such as the Yao, Bisa, Lunda and Imbangala (Map 10) were joined by the Kamba, Nyamwezi, Ovimbundu, and after 1850 by the Cokwe. These traders dealt in articles which were in short supply in the interior, such as salt, iron and copper. They also conveyed ivory and slaves to the coast. The most successful were the Nyamwezi and the Cokwe. Both of them gained political control of large areas where they had begun as traders. Msiri's Nyamwezi (or 'Yeke') state was situated in Katanga, more than 800 kilometres from the Nyamwezi homeland.

The coastal traders fall into three main groups:

a) The *pombeiros* (Map 10) advanced inland from both Angola and Mozambique. Between 1805 and 1815 they crossed the continent from west to east.

b) The Arabs and Swahili of the East African coast were the most influential of all. Partly on account of the commercial ambitions of Sayyid Said of Zanzibar they began in the 1830s to traverse the routes of the Yao, Nyamwezi and Kamba. On Lake Malawi and at Tabora they established strong, independent bases, while on the Lualaba Tippu Tib created a vast state linked commercially to the East African coast (1875–90).

c) The 'Khartoumers' (or Sudanese) were not strictly speaking from the coast, but they supplied the ivory markets of Egypt, and they represented a particularly destructive penetration by the outside world. From about 1850–83 they were active in the regions round Lake Albert, as well as further north in the Southern Sudan. They alone may be said to have opened up a new trade route.

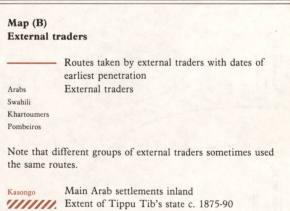

Key to maps

Map (A)
Trading peoples of the interior

———— Trade routes opened up by the peoples of the interior

COKWE — Peoples who took part in long-distance trade
NYAMWEZI
KAMBA
BISA
YAO
OVIMBUNDU
IMBANGALA
FANG
TEKE
LUNDA

The names over the trade routes give a rough idea which traders traversed which routes. Note, however, that two or more peoples sometimes used the same route, and that there was considerable variation during this period.

▨▨▨ Land over 2,000 m

Map (B)
External traders

———— Routes taken by external traders with dates of earliest penetration

Arabs — External traders
Swahili
Khartoumers
Pombeiros

Note that different groups of external traders sometimes used the same routes.

Kasongo — Main Arab settlements inland

▨▨▨ Extent of Tippu Tib's state c. 1875-90

▨▨▨ Land over 2,000 m

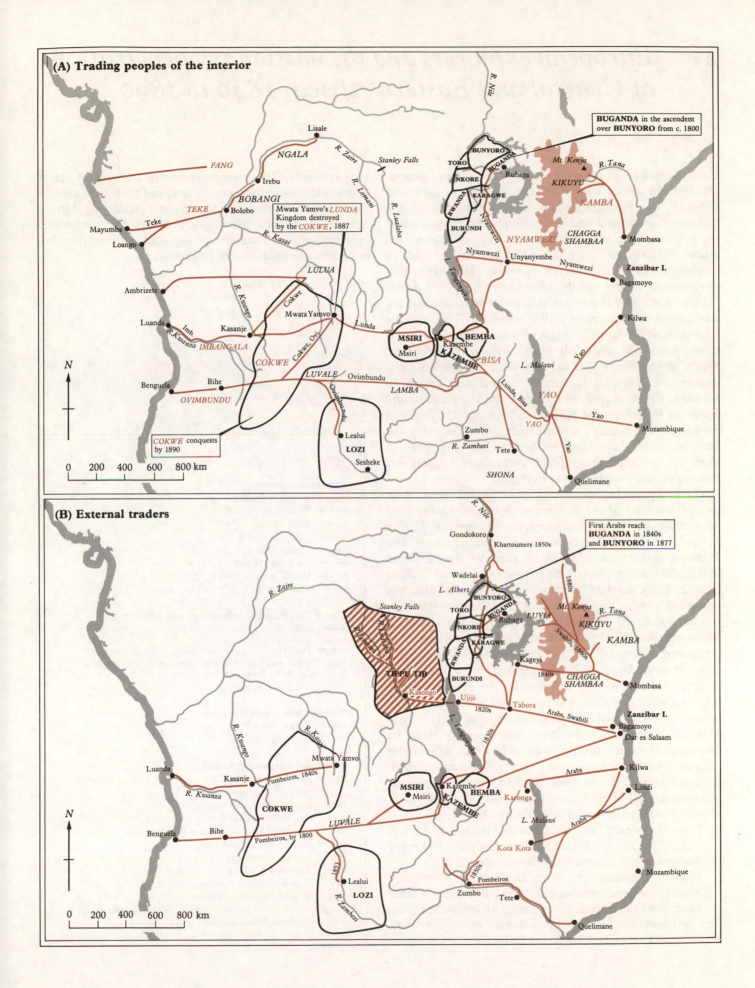

(A) Trading peoples of the interior

FANG

NGALA
Lisale
R. Zaire
Stanley Falls
R. Lomani

BUGANDA in the ascendent
over BUNYORO from c. 1800

BUNYORO
TORO BUGANDA
NKORE Rubaga
KARAGWE
Mt. Kenya R. Tana
KIKUYU
KAMBA

Irebu
BOBANGI
TEKE
Bolobo
R. Lualaba

Mayumba
Teke
RWANDA

Loango
BURUNDI
NYAMWEZI
CHAGGA
SHAMBAA
Mombasa

Mwata Yamvo's *LUNDA*
Kingdom destroyed
by the *COKWE*, 1887

R. Kasai

LULUA
Nyamwezi
Unyanyembe Nyamwezi
Zanzibar I.

Ambrizete
R. Kwango
Cokwe
Mwata Yamvo

Bagamoyo

Luanda
Imb.
R. Kwanza
Kasanje
IMBANGALA
Cokwe, Ovi.
Lunda
MSIRI
Msiri Kazembe
BEMBA
KAZEMBE
L. Malawi
Kilwa
Yao

N
COKWE
LUVALE Ovimbundu
LAMBA
Lunda, Bisa
YAO

Benguela
Bihe
OVIMBUNDU
Ovimbundu
Zumbo
YAO
Yao
Mozambique

COKWE conquests
by 1890
Lealui
R. Zambezi
Tete

0 200 400 600 800 km
LOZI
Sesheke
SHONA
Quelimane

(B) External traders

R. Nile
Gondokoro
Khartoumers 1850s

R. Zaire
Wadelai
1880s
L. Albert
BUNYORO
LUYIA
Mt. Kenya R. Tana

First Arabs reach
BUGANDA in 1840s
and BUNYORO in 1877

Stanley Falls
R. Lualaba
TORO BUGANDA
NKORE Rubaga
KIKUYU
KAMBA

R. Lomani
RWANDA
KARAGWE
Kageyi
Swahili, 1860s

TIPPU TIB
BURUNDI
1840s
CHAGGA
SHAMBAA
Mombasa

Kasongo
Ujiji
1820s
Tabora
Arabs, Swahili

R. Kwango
R. Kasai
1830s
Zanzibar I.
Bagamoyo
Dar es Salaam

Luanda
Kasanje
Mwata Yamvo
Pombeiros, 1840s
Arabs
Kilwa
Lindi

R. Kwanza
COKWE
MSIRI
Msiri Kazembe
BEMBA
KAZEMBE
Karonga

N
LUVALE
L. Malawi
Arabs

Benguela
Bihe
Pombeiros, by 1800
Kota Kota

1853
Mozambique
1850s
Pombeiros
Zumbo
Tete

0 200 400 600 800 km
Lealui
R. Zambezi
LOZI
Quelimane

European explorers and the missionary penetration of Central and Eastern Africa, 1840 to 1890

Until the mid 19th century, Europe's knowledge of Central and Eastern Africa was effectively confined to the coast, although the Portuguese had some knowledge of the hinterland of Angola and Mozambique. Europeans could see little purpose in braving the hazards of exploration inland. What caused them to modify their attitude was an awakening of humanitarian concern. However, this concern was at first mainly directed towards West Africa (Maps 16 and 18). It was not until the 1850s that attention was turned to other parts of the continent. This was the achievement of David Livingstone who between 1854 and 1856 crossed the continent from Luanda to Quelimane. Much of this route had actually been traversed by the Portuguese, but Livingstone's appeal for action to eradicate the slave trade of Central Africa had a profound effect on British public opinion. There quickly followed the journeys of Burton, Speke, Grant and Baker. After the descent of the Zaire river by Stanley (an American) in 1876–77, the main geographical features of Central and Eastern Africa were known to Europe.

The first people to take advantage of the discoveries were the missionaries of the Protestant churches. Livingstone himself was a Scottish missionary, his base originally being in South Africa. Missions were established by the Presbyterians on Lake Malawi in 1876, by the Anglicans in Buganda in 1877, and by the Baptists on the middle Zaire in 1882. The Catholic Church soon followed, with missions opened in 1879 in Buganda and on Lake Tanganyika.

The impact of the missionaries varied considerably. Many of them tried to build up Christian communities composed of freed slaves and other refugees; individual converts could be made by this method, but at the cost of leaving African society unaffected. By contrast, some missions were established at the courts of strong African rulers (e.g. Mutesa of Buganda, Lewanika of the Lozi, and Msiri of Katanga), in the hope that a society could be converted from the top. But these rulers were often more interested in the diplomatic and technical assistance which the missionaries could provide than in their spiritual message. Only in two African states had the missionaries achieved a large number of converts by 1890:

a) Buganda, where both the Church Missionary Society (Anglican) and the White Fathers (Catholic) had made many converts among the political elite;

b) Imerina (Madagascar), where the London Missionary Society (inter-denominational) had been active since 1820, the Prime Minister becoming a Christian in 1868.

Few missionaries advocated colonial rule, but their activities did have a bearing on the European partition from 1875 onwards. The missionaries were a source of scarce information about local conditions; and they were used by their home governments to support 'claims' to African territory. It was only after colonial rule had been extended over most of Africa that the missionaries achieved their full impact on spiritual life and education.

Key to map

European explorers

━━━	Burton & Speke 1857-9
━·━	Speke & Grant 1862-3
⋯⋯	Baker 1863-4
────	Cameron 1873-4
━ ━	Stanley 1874-7
━·─	De Brazza 1875-9
─ ─ ─	Von Wissmann 1880-3
⋯⋯⋯	Thomson 1883

David Livingstone – missionary and explorer

────	1853-56
⋯⋯⋯	1859-64
━ ━	1867-73

Note: On this map only the most important of the countless journeys made by Europeans are shown.

─ ─ ─	'Stevenson Road'

Catholic Missionary Societies

HGF	Holy Ghost Fathers
WF	White Fathers

Protestant Missionary Societies

ABC	American Board of Commissions for Foreign Missions (mainly Congregationalist)
BMS	Baptist Missionary Society
CMS	Church Missionary Society (Anglican)
CSM	Church of Scotland Mission (Presbyterian)
FCS	Free Church of Scotland
LMS	London Missionary Society
PB	Plymouth Brethren
PEM	Paris Evangelical Mission
RMS	Rhenish Missionary Society
UMCA	Universities Mission to Central Africa (Anglican)
WMS	Wesleyan Missionary Society

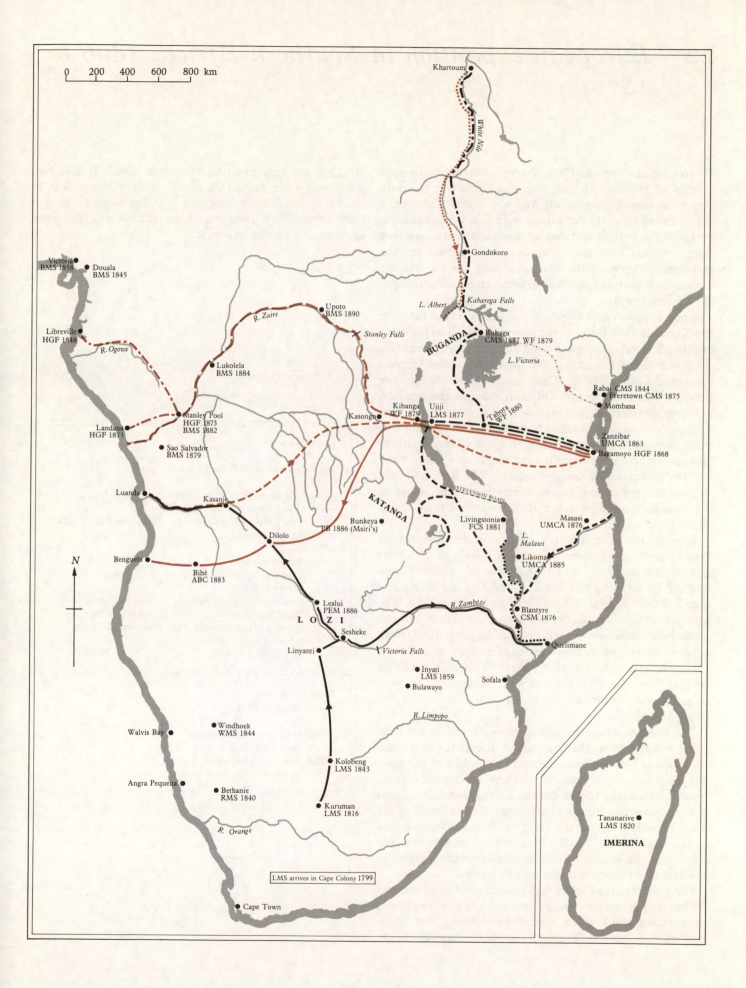

0 200 400 600 800 km

Khartoum

White Nile

Gondokoro

L. Albert *Kabarega Falls*

Victoria
BMS 1858

Douala
BMS 1845

BUGANDA

Rubaga
CMS 1877 WF 1879

L. Victoria

Libreville
HGF 1848

R. Zaire

Upoto
BMS 1890

Stanley Falls

Rabai CMS 1844
Freretown CMS 1875

Mombasa

R. Ogowe

Lukolela
BMS 1884

Kibanga
WF 1879

Ujiji
LMS 1877

Tabora
WF 1880

Zanzibar
UMCA 1863

Stanley Pool
HGF 1873
BMS 1882

Kasongo

Bagamoyo HGF 1868

Landana
HGF 1873

Sao Salvador
BMS 1879

Luanda

Kasanje

KATANGA

STEVENSON ROAD

Livingstonia
FCS 1881

Masasi
UMCA 1876

Dilolo

Bunkeya
PB 1886 (Msiri's)

*L.
Malawi*

Benguela

Bihé
ABC 1883

Likoma
UMCA 1885

N

Lealui
PEM 1886

R. Zambezi

Blantyre
CSM 1876

LOZI

Sesheke

Quelimane

Linyanti

Victoria Falls

Inyati
LMS 1859

Bulawayo

Sofala

R. Limpopo

Walvis Bay

Windhoek
WMS 1844

Angra Pequena

Bethanie
RMS 1840

Kolobeng
LMS 1843

Tananarive
LMS 1820

IMERINA

Kuruman
LMS 1816

R. Orange

LMS arrives in Cape Colony 1799

Cape Town

22   *European expansion in Southern Africa, 1806 to 1870*

From 1806 onwards the Cape was under the uninterrupted control of Britain. At that time the Cape was the only colony in what is now South Africa, but this was not the case for very long. By 1870 there were four white colonies, two of them British and two of them under independent Boer control. The main themes in this period are the relationship between the two colonising stocks, and the increasingly stormy relationship between the colonists and the African peoples.

Since 1779 war had been intermittently waged between the Xhosa and the Boers of the eastern Cape. The presence of British regular troops from 1811 gave the colonists a decisive military advantage. But the British did not intend to extend Cape Colony. They wanted a stable frontier between white and black. On both sides of the frontier, however, population pressure worked against this policy. The problem was intensified because the Boers wanted as little as possible to do with British ideas of race relations and law enforcement; they tended to advance beyond any frontier laid down by the government. The British sought to stop this expansion, and to strengthen their control of the frontier zone by placing British settlers there (from 1820 onwards).

This was the background of the large-scale emigration of Boers from Cape Colony in 1836–38 known as the Great Trek. The intention was to by-pass the eastern Cape frontier by trekking north across the Orange River, and thence either to Natal (the majority) or the High Veld. The Mfecane (Map 19) had depopulated many areas, but the trekkers nevertheless were confronted by powerful African adversaries who were only defeated after heavy white losses – the Ndebele at Marico (1837) and the Zulu at Blood River (1838). The Boers then set about establishing pioneer farming communities in Natal and west of the Drakensberg.

The reaction of the British authorities was for the time being to leave the trekkers unmolested, with the important exception of Natal. The existence of a republic on the coast was believed to threaten the safety of Britain's communications in the Indian Ocean. Troops were landed and in 1843 Natal was annexed by Britain. By 1849 most of the Boers there had left for the High Veld, and British settlers replaced them in Natal. Meanwhile, under Mpande (1840–72), the adjacent Zulu kingdom pursued a policy of peaceful coexistence with the British colony.

For a short period (1848–54) Britain tried to administer the Boers between the Orange and the Vaal, but in 1852 and 1854 conventions were signed recognising the independence of both the Transvaal and the Orange Free State.

By 1870 the only practical limitation which Britain had placed on Boer expansion north of the Orange was to annex Moshoeshoe's kingdom (as Basutoland). It was only events after 1870 which set Britain and the Boer republics on a collision course.

Key to map

→   Main routes of Great Trek, with leaders

— —   1829 boundary of Cape Colony
– – –   1847 boundary of Cape Colony
|||||||| Land conquered by Orange Free State from Basuto 1866
ZULU   African peoples

White colonies:
Transvaal: from 1860, South African Republic
Orange Free State
Basutoland: formerly Lesotho, annexed by Britain in 1869
Natal: Boer republic, 1838-43, British colony from 1843
Queen Adelaide Province: 1834-36; British Kaffraria, 1847;
to Cape Colony, 1865
Portuguese East Africa

Key to map inset
South Africa in 1870

\\\\\   Areas under British control
▦   Areas under Boer control
▬   Areas under Portuguese control
////   Areas still independent of colonial rule

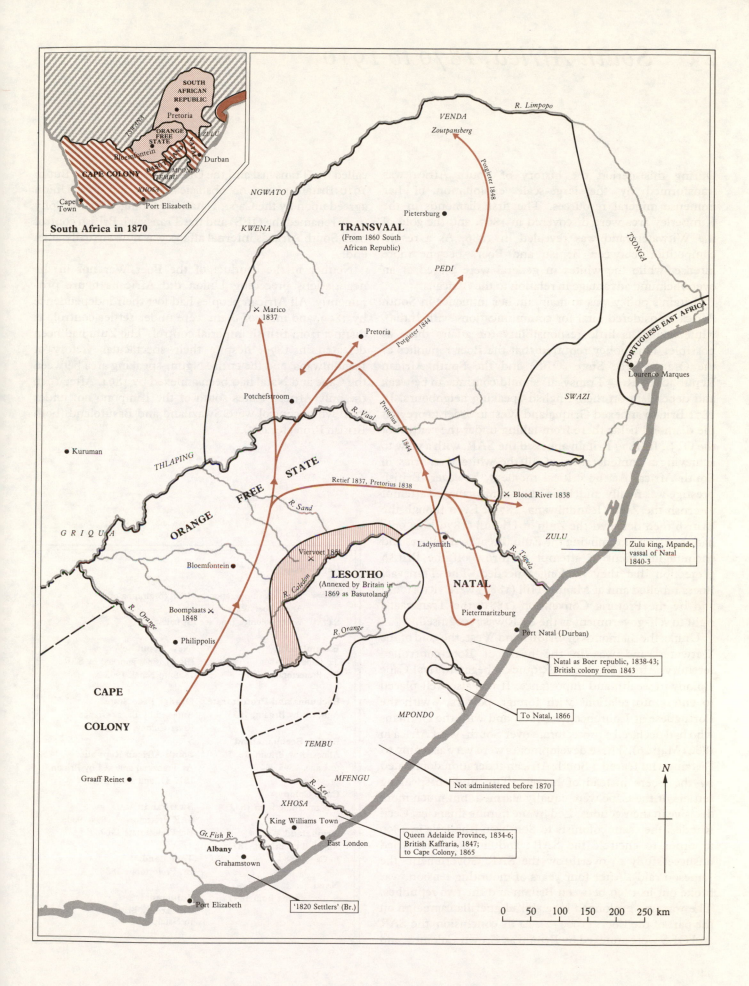

South Africa in 1870

SOUTH
AFRICAN
REPUBLIC
Pretoria
TSWANA
ORANGE
FREE
STATE
Bloemfontein
ZULU
BASUTO
NATAL
Durban
CAPE COLONY
MPONDO
TEMBU
Cape
Town
XHOSA
Port Elizabeth

R. Limpopo

VENDA
Zoutpansberg

Potgieter 1848

Pietersburg

TRANSVAAL
(From 1860 South
African Republic)

PEDI

NGWATO

KWENA

TSONGA

PORTUGUESE EAST AFRICA

Lourenço Marques

SWAZI

× Marico
1837

Pretoria

Potgieter 1844

Potchefstroom

R. Vaal

Pretorius 1844

Kuruman

THLAPING

ORANGE   FREE   STATE

R. Sand

Retief 1837, Pretorius 1838

× Blood River 1838

ZULU

Ladysmith

R. Tugela

Zulu king, Mpande,
vassal of Natal
1840-3

GRIQUA

Vieryoet 1851 ×

Bloemfontein •

R. Caledon

LESOTHO
(Annexed by Britain in
1869 as Basutoland)

R. Orange

NATAL

Pietermaritzburg

Boomplaats ×
1848

Philippolis •

R. Orange

Port Natal (Durban)

R. Orange

Natal as Boer republic, 1838-43;
British colony from 1843

CAPE

COLONY

MPONDO

To Natal, 1866

TEMBU

MFENGU

Not administered before 1870

Graaff Reinet •

R. Kei

XHOSA

King Williams Town

Gt. Fish R.

East London

Queen Adelaide Province, 1834-6;
British Kaffraria, 1847;
to Cape Colony, 1865

Albany
Grahamstown

Port Elizabeth

'1820 Settlers' (Br.)

0   50   100   150   200   250 km

N

During this period the history of South Africa was transformed by the large-scale exploitation of her immense mineral resources. The first diamonds in the Kimberley area were discovered in 1867, and the gold of the Witwatersrand was revealed in 1886. As a result, competition between British and Boers became more intense, while the whites in general were placed at an overwhelming advantage in relation to the Africans.

Britain's policy was to maintain her influence in South Africa (considered vital for communications with India), while taking as little responsibility for affairs there as possible. This policy required that the Boer republics of the Orange Free State (OFS) and the South African Republic (SAR, = Transvaal) should continue to be weak and dependent on their English-speaking neighbours. In 1871 Britain annexed Griqualand West in order to prevent the diamond fields there from falling under the control of the OFS. In 1877 Britain annexed the SAR, with a view to achieving a confederation of all the white territories in South Africa. At the critical moment, however, British prestige was fatally undermined by a mismanaged attempt to crush the Zulu (Isandhlwana, 1879). Even though the British then defeated the Zulu at Ulundi (1879) this only had the effect of removing the Zulu threat to the Boers and encouraging them to attempt to throw off the British protection that they no longer needed. The Transvaal Boers rebelled and at Majuba Hill (1881) were victorious; and by the Pretoria Convention (1881) the Transvaal's right to self-government as the SAR was recognised.

Unlike the diamonds of Griqualand West, the gold of the Witwatersrand was in the heart of Boer-controlled territory. After 1886 the SAR quickly began to rival Cape Colony in wealth and importance. It was also well-placed to enter into relations with foreign powers – with the Portuguese at Lourenco Marques, and with the Germans who had declared a protectorate over South-West Africa in 1884 (Map 26). These developments were very alarming to Britain, who feared a South African federation dominated by the Boers instead of herself. The English-speaking settlers of the Cape were equally alarmed, but much more decisive in their actions. Led by the mining financier, Cecil Rhodes, they sent colonists to Southern Rhodesia in 1890 in order to encircle the SAR; and in 1895 they tried unsuccessfully to overthrow the SAR Government (the Jameson raid). After four years of mounting tension, war broke out in 1899 between Britain and the two republics. The war was prolonged by a skilful guerilla campaign on the part of the Boers (1900–2). At its conclusion, the SAR and OFS were annexed by Britain as Crown Colonies (and called the Transvaal and the Orange River Colony). But in 1910 Britain placed no obstacles in the way of a Union agreed upon by the Cape, Natal, the Orange River Colony (now renamed the OFS) and the Transvaal. British control over South Africa's internal affairs was now virtually at an end.

Neither in the conduct of the Boer War nor in the negotiations preceding Union did Africans figure prominently. All African peoples had lost their independence by 1899, and most of them were under settler control, as distinct from British imperial control. The Zulu had been defeated in 1879, despite their spectacular victory at Isandhlwana, and the entire Nguni-speaking area between the Cape and Natal had been annexed by 1894. After 1910 the only African states south of the Limpopo not under local white control were Swaziland and Basutoland (both British Protectorates).

Key to map

━━━ Railways in operation by 1899 (beginning of Anglo-Boer War)

NATAL White colonies (and see list below)

Basutoland
To Cape 1871-84;
Br. Protectorate 1884

Bechuanaland Protectorate
Annexed by Britain, 1885

British Bechuanaland
Annexed by Britain, 1885;
to Cape, 1895

Cape Colony:
Self-governing from 1872

Griqualand West
Annexed by Britain, 1871;
to Cape, 1880

Natal
Self-governing from 1893

'New Republic'
(Boer) 1884; annexed by SAR, 1888; to Natal, 1902

Orange Free State
Annexed by Br. as Orange River Colony, 1902

South African Republic:
As Transvaal annexed by Britain, 1877-81, and again in 1902

Swaziland:
SAR Protectorate, 1894-1900; Br. Protectorate 1907

Tongaland:
Br. Protectorate 1888

Zululand:
Annexed by Britain 1887; to Natal, 1897

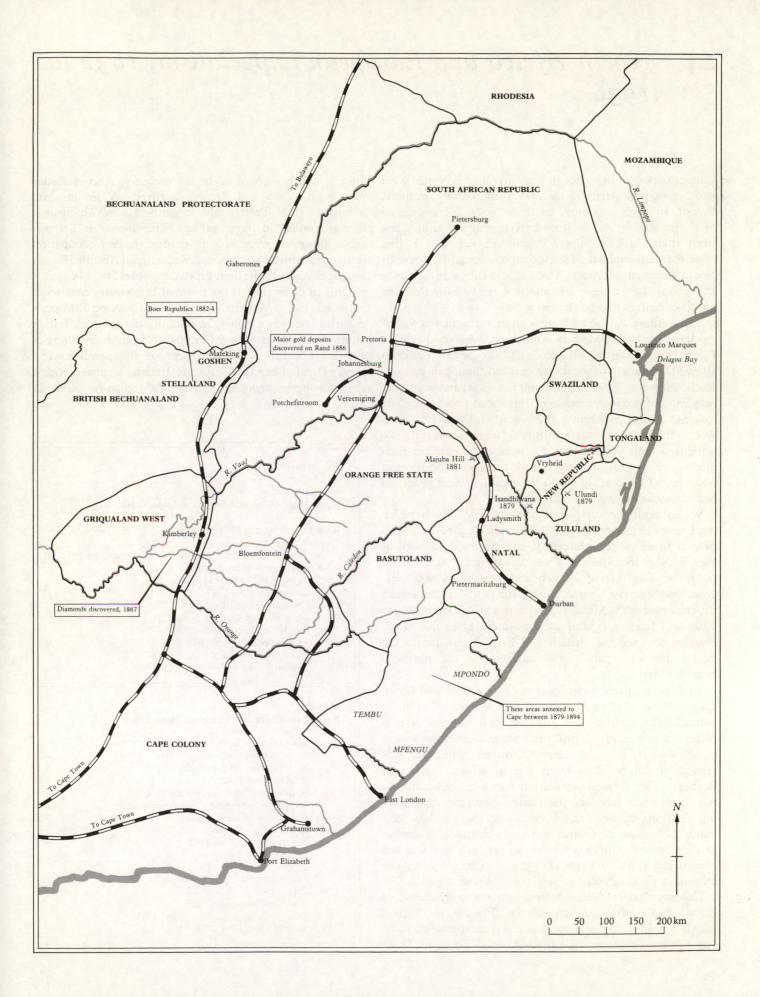

RHODESIA

MOZAMBIQUE

SOUTH AFRICAN REPUBLIC

BECHUANALAND PROTECTORATE

Pietersburg

To Bulawayo

Gaberones

R. Limpopo

Boer Republics 1882-4

GOSHEN

Mafeking

Pretoria

Lourenco Marques

Delagoa Bay

Major gold deposits
discovered on Rand 1886

STELLALAND

Johannesburg

SWAZILAND

BRITISH BECHUANALAND

Potchefstroom

Vereeniging

TONGALAND

R. Vaal

ORANGE FREE STATE

Majuba Hill
1881

Vryheid

NEW REPUBLIC

GRIQUALAND WEST

Isandhlwana
1879

Ulundi
1879

Kimberley

Ladysmith

ZULULAND

Bloemfontein

R. Caledon

BASUTOLAND

NATAL

Diamonds discovered, 1867

Pietermaritzburg

Durban

R. Orange

MPONDO

These areas annexed to
Cape between 1879-1894

TEMBU

CAPE COLONY

MFENGU

To Cape Town

N

To Cape Town

East London

To Cape Town

Grahamstown

Port Elizabeth

0   50   100   150   200km

24 North Africa and European imperialism, 1832 to 1936

European powers first became fully involved in North-West and North-East Africa in the mid-19th century. Initially, except in Algeria, they tried to secure commercial privileges and to buy or lease harbours and trading posts from their African rulers. Private French and Italian businessmen established connections along the coast of North Africa, in Morocco, Tunisia, and Libya, in the 1850s and 1860s. Later, their operations spread to the Red Sea coasts of Eritrea and Somaliland.

Some rulers welcomed European investment as a way of modernising their countries. Mohammed Ali and Ismail in Egypt, the Sultans of Morocco, and the Bey of Tunis all allowed foreigners to settle and granted them concessions. In the long run, however, attempts at social and economic reform, and the interference of European powers in their internal affairs, weakened these states. Their treasuries were emptied and their subjects were in revolt. To safeguard their investments, European governments then intervened – first in Egypt and then in Tunisia and Morocco. This quickly led to the establishment of formal protectorates and spheres of influence.

Wider strategic considerations and rivalries between the European powers during the 'Scramble for Africa' also helped to shape the pattern of colonial rule. Control of Egypt and of the Nile valley was considered vital to British interests. The fear of French and Belgian (Congo) encroachment on the Upper Nile led the British to undertake the conquest of the Mahdist state in the Sudan from 1896 to 1899 and later to extend their boundaries in the south. Rivalry between the British and French also led to the declaration of separate protectorates on the northern Somali coast.

In Algeria, French occupation came earlier and lasted longer. From 1832 to the 1880s the French army gradually extended its control over the Algerian interior despite bitter resistance. Here, European economic interests were established by force. A large European population was settled on lands taken from the Muslims, Arabs and Berbers. This foreign population was a crucial factor in Algerian history from conquest to independence, embittering relations between the French and the Muslims and making eventual decolonisation more difficult. A similar process occurred in Tripolitania, where Italy first wrested control from the Turks (1911–13) and then conquered the inhabitants and established settler villages on their land.

Colonisation was resisted strongly in many areas. Abd-el Kader led resistance against the French in Algeria (1832–47) in a struggle to create an independent state. After initial successes, culminating in the Treaty of Tafna

(1837), which recognised his sovereignty, Abd-el Kader was worn down and finally captured. A similar fate attended Arabi Pasha, who organised a revolt against foreign control in Egypt (1882). The Sanusi in Tripolitania, however, were able to contest Italian occupation until 1932; and Somalis under Mohammed Abdille Hassan fought British and Italians for twenty years (1899–1920).

Only in Ethiopia was the trend of European penetration reversed. Here, Menelik II was able to play on European rivalries. At Adwa (1896) he soundly defeated an Italian attempt to expand on to the highlands from their colony of Eritrea. Thereafter, Ethiopia kept her independence and even extended her rule until the Italians returned with a greatly superior army and crushed Ethiopian resistance in 1936.

Key to maps

Map (A)
North-West Africa and European imperialism

→ Main routes of French advance:
Tunisia: Protectorate 1883
Morocco: Partitioned 1904-12; French Protectorate 1912
--→ Main routes of Italian advance:
Tripolitania: Conquered 1929
Fezzan: Conquered 1931
Cyrenaica: Conquered 1931-2
Main areas occupied by Spain:
Rio de Oro: Sp. occupation 1884
Spanish Sahara: Protectorate 1912
Ifni: Protectorate 1860
Spanish Morocco: Protectorate 1909-56

Map (B)
North-East Africa and European imperialism

→ Main routes of British advance:
Egypt: Anglo-French control 1876;
Br. occupation 1882; protectorate 1914;
self-government 1922
British Somaliland: protectorate 1884
Sudan: Anglo-Egyptian Condominium 1899
--→ Main routes of Italian advance:
Assab: Private company 1870; Italian
Government purchase 1882
Danakil Coast: Protectorate 1885
Eritrea: Protectorate 1889
Italian Somaliland: Protectorate 1889;
Colony 1905
Ethiopia: Conquered 1936
Defeats: Dogali 1887, Amba Alagi 1895,
Mekelle 1896, Adwa 1896

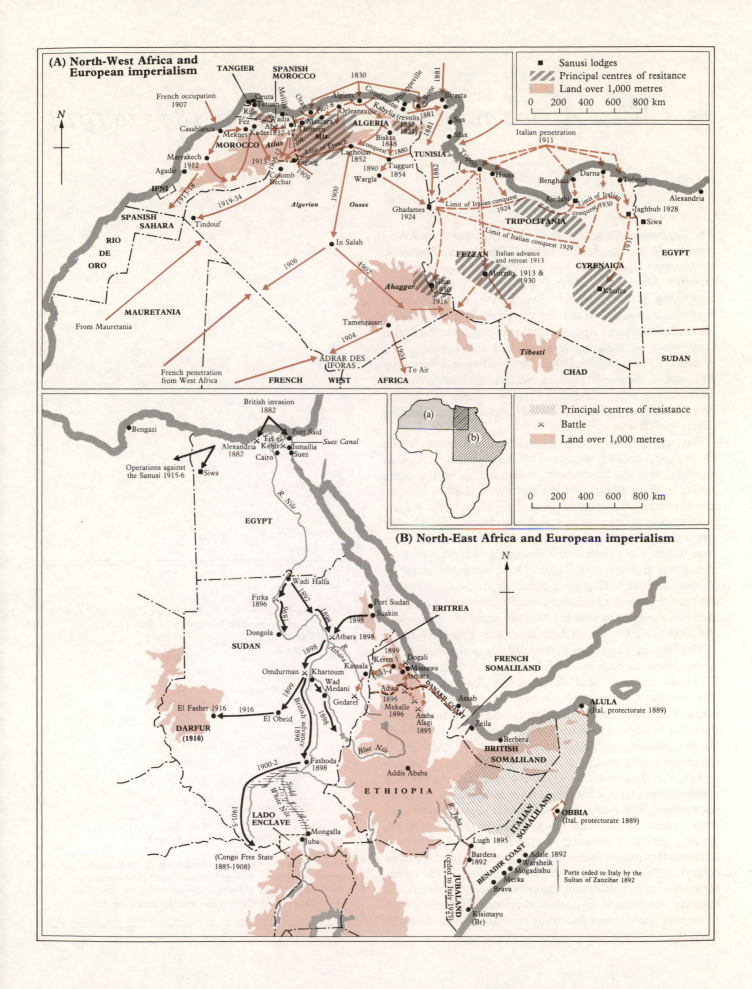

(A) North-West Africa and European imperialism

Legend:
- ■ Sanusi lodges
- ▨ Principal centres of resistance
- Land over 1,000 metres
- 0 200 400 600 800 km

N

TANGIER
SPANISH MOROCCO
French occupation 1907
Ceuta
Melilla
Tetuan
Rif
Fez
Abd al
Kader 1832-47
Oran
1907-8
Algiers
Constantine
Philippeville
Bone
1881
Bizerta
1830
Casablanca
Meknes
Mascara
Tlemcen
1908-13
ALGERIA
Kabylia (revolts 1857, 1871)
1881
Sus
MOROCCO
Atlas Mts.
1905-12
line of French
Biskra
1848
1881
Sfax
Marrakech 1912
Figuig
Laghouat
1852
conquest
1880
TUNISIA
Italian penetration 1911
Agadir
1913
Colomb Bechar
1909
1890
Tuggurt 1854
1882
Tripoli
Homs
Benghazi
Darna
Tobruq
IFNI
1913-18
Wargla
Ghadames 1924
Ajedabi
Limit of Italian conquest 1930
Jaghbub 1928
Alexandria
1919-34
Limit of Italian conquest 1924
Siwa
SPANISH SAHARA
Tindouf
Algerian
Oases
TRIPOLITANIA
RIO DE ORO
1906
In Salah
Limit of Italian conquest 1929
EGYPT
MAURETANIA
1902
FEZZAN
Italian advance and retreat 1913
CYRENAICA
From Mauretania
Ahaggar
Ghat 1930
Murzuq 1913 & 1930
Khufra
1916
Tamenrasset
1904
Tibesti
ADRAR DES IFORAS
1904
To Air
SUDAN
French penetration from West Africa
FRENCH WEST AFRICA
CHAD

Inset legend:
- ▨ Principal centres of resistance
- × Battle
- Land over 1,000 metres
- 0 200 400 600 800 km

(B) North-East Africa and European imperialism

N

Bengazi
British invasion 1882
Port Said
Suez Canal
Alexandria 1882
Tel el Kebir
Ismailia
Operations against the Sanusi 1915-6
Siwa
Cairo
Suez
EGYPT
R. Nile
Wadi Halfa
1897
Firka 1896
Port Sudan
Suakin
ERITREA
1896
1898
Atbara 1898
1899
Keren
Dogali
Dongola
1898
R. Atbara
Kassala
1883-4
Massawa
Asmara
FRENCH SOMALILAND
SUDAN
Omdurman
Khartoum
Wad Medani
Adwa 1896
Mekalle 1896
Assab
DANAKIL COAST
ALULA (Ital. protectorate 1889)
El Fasher 1916
1916
El Obeid
Gedaref
Amba Alagi 1895
Zeila
British advance 1898
1899
1898
Blue Nile
Berbera
DARFUR (1916)
Fashoda 1898
Addis Ababa
BRITISH SOMALILAND
ITALIAN SOMALILAND
1900-2
ETHIOPIA
OBBIA (Ital. protectorate 1889)
1901-5
Sudd
White Nile
LADO ENCLAVE
Mongalla
Juba
R. Juba
Lugh 1895
(Congo Free State 1885-1908)
JUBALAND (ceded to Italy 1925)
Bardera 1892
Adale 1892
BENADIR COAST
Warsheik
Mogadishu
Merka
Brava
Ports ceded to Italy by the Sultan of Zanzibar 1892
Kisimayu (Br)

25   *West Africa and European partition, 1875 to 1914*

The beginning of the European partition was moulded by two men: Leopold II, King of the Belgians, and Bismarck, the German Chancellor. The activities of Leopold and the explorer Stanley in lower Zaire from 1877, and the competing activities of de Brazza for France, led to conflicting imperial claims. By the time these claims were reconciled and given international recognition at the Berlin Conference of 1884–5, Germany had also joined in the Scramble. For reasons of domestic politics and European diplomacy, Bismarck made a sudden bid for colonies: protectorates were declared in Togo, Kamerun and South-West Africa just before the Berlin Conference, and in East Africa just after it.

The arrival of two new colonial powers on the scene forced the hand of powers with long-standing African interests, and the Scramble now entered its most intense phase. In West Africa, Britain and France had to advance into the interior in order to secure the hinterlands of their existing coastal colonies and trading ports and avoid losing markets of their manufactured goods to the Germans or to each other. For example the British speeded up making protection treaties with Niger Delta states in order to forestall a possible German advance from the Cameroons; the trader George Goldie and his Royal Niger Company made similar treaties with the Muslim emirs of the interior; and in 1885 Britain set up the Niger Coast Protectorate.

The Berlin Conference speeded up colonisation by laying down the principle of 'effective occupation' before a European country could claim to rule African territory. The Berlin Conference required that each European country claiming a piece of African land should inform all the other European countries who signed the act produced by the conference. This meant that any of these other countries would also be able to make their claims to this territory if they had any. Once a European country had claimed some land it then had to make good its claim by occupation. Europeans hurriedly made protection treaties with rulers whose land they desired. These treaties, actually giving or claiming to give Europeans rights over African territories, were often signed without African rulers realising what they meant. In many areas rulers refused to sign treaties and Europeans were forced to send military expeditions to impose their rule. The resistance put up by these rulers and their communities is shown in Map 28.

Key to map

▨	Areas occupied by the colonial powers before the Partition
Lagos	Trading posts held by the colonial powers before the Partition
	French
	St. Louis
	Dakar
	Grand Bassam
	Porto Novo
	British
	Bathurst
	Freetown
	Cape Coast
	Accra
	Lagos
	Portuguese
	Bissao
1886	Colonial frontiers, with date of fixing
→	Main routes of British advance during the Partition
→	Main routes of French advance during the Partition
⇢	Main routes of German advance during the Partition
⇢	Main route of Portuguese advance during the Partition

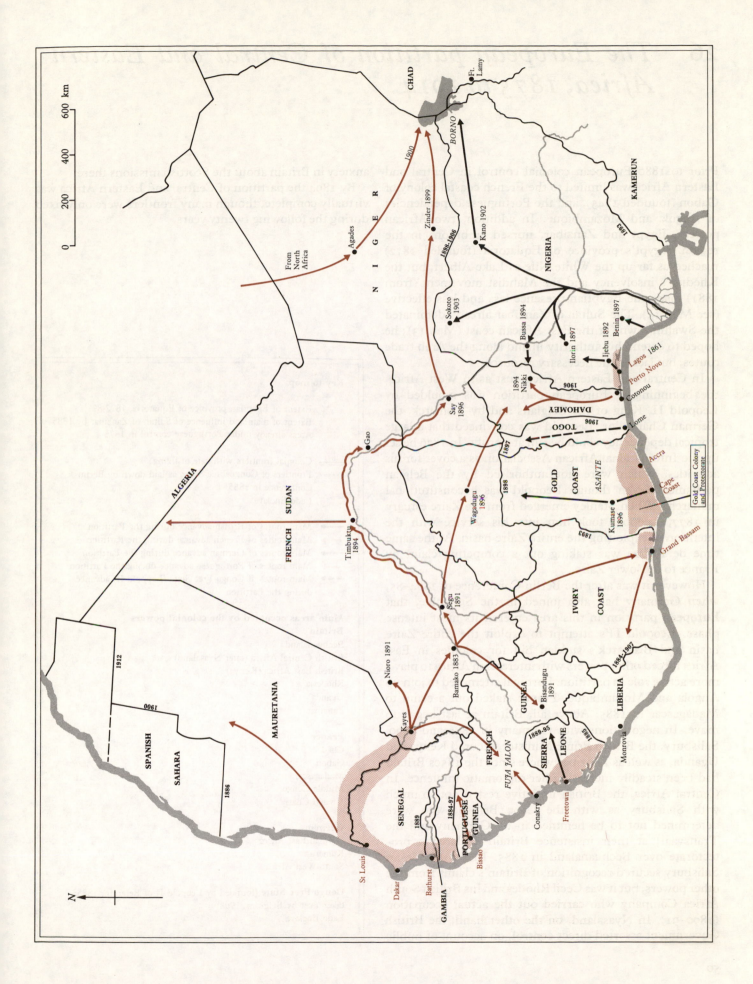

CHAD

Ft. Lamy

KAMERUN

1883

BORNO

NIGER

Kano 1902

NIGERIA

From North Africa

Agades

Zinder 1899

1898-1906

Sokoto 1903

Bussa 1894

Benin 1897

Ilorin 1897

Jebu 1892

Lagos 1861

Porto Novo

Cotonou

Lome

Nikki 1894

1906

DAHOMEY

1906

TOGO

1897

Say 1896

Accra

GOLD COAST

ASANTE

Cape Coast

Gao

Wagadugu 1896

1898

Gold Coast Colony and Protectorate

Kumase 1896

1893

Timbuktu 1894

ALGERIA

FRENCH SUDAN

Grand Bassam

Segu 1891

IVORY COAST

Nioro 1891

Bamako 1883

Bisandugu 1891

GUINEA

LIBERIA

1884-1907

Kayes

FRENCH GUINEA

FUTA JALON

1889-95

1885

Monrovia

MAURETANIA

1912

1900

SPANISH SAHARA

1886

SENEGAL

1889

1884-97

PORTUGUESE GUINEA

SIERRA LEONE

Conakry

Freetown

St Louis

Dakar

Bathurst

Bissao

GAMBIA

N

km
600
400
200
0

26 The European partition of Central and Eastern Africa, 1875 to 1914

Prior to 1880 European colonial control in Central and Eastern Africa was limited to the French coastal colony of Gabon (founded 1845), and the Portuguese dependencies of Angola and Mozambique. In addition, two African powers, Egypt and Zanzibar, nursed ambitions in the region. Egypt's province of Equatoria (founded 1872) reached as far up the White Nile as Lake Albert, but the Khedive's insolvency and the Mahdist movement (from 1881) made the Egyptian presence less and less effective (see Map 15). The Sultan of Zanzibar already dominated the Swahili towns of the East African coast (Map 13); he hoped to extend his authority inland along the Arab trade routes, but lacked the necessary resources.

In Central and Eastern Africa, just as in West Africa, the beginning of European partition was moulded by Leopold II, King of the Belgians and by Bismarck, the German Chancellor. Leopold was convinced that a large tropical dependency could be run at a profit. In 1876 he set up the International African Association as a cover for his activities, which were not authorised by the Belgian parliament (even though Leopold was a constitutional monarch). When Stanley emerged from the Zaire estuary in 1877, Leopold took him into his service with the intention of exploiting the entire Zaire basin. At the same time de Brazza was staking out a competing claim by France to the lower Zaire.

However it was after the Berlin Conference of 1884–85, when Germany had also joined in the Scramble, that European partition in this area entered its most intense phase. Leopold II's attempt to exploit the entire Zaire basin and Bismarck's sudden bid for colonies in East Africa forced other powers with interests in Africa to play a more active role in partition. Portugal attempted to join up Angola and Mozambique. France staked out a claim to Madagascar in 1885. Above all, Britain at last began to move. In negotiations with Germany in 1886 and 1890, Salisbury, the British Prime Minister, secured Kenya and Uganda, as well as Zanzibar where since the 1850s Britain had been steadily increasing her diplomatic influence. In Central Africa, the British initiative rested not so much with Salisbury as with the Cape British, who were determined not to be hemmed in by Germany and the Transvaal; at their insistence Britain declared a protectorate over Bechuanaland in 1885. In the Rhodesias Salisbury secured recognition of Britain's claims from the other powers, but it was Cecil Rhodes and his British South Africa Company who carried out the actual occupation (1890–91). In Nyasaland, on the other hand, the British Government asserted direct control, on account of public anxiety in Britain about the Scottish missions there.

By 1894 the partition of Central and Eastern Africa was virtually complete, though many frontiers were only fixed during the following twenty years.

Key to map

///// Extent of Egyptian province of Equatoria, 1872-89

▧ Extent of mainland influence of Sultan of Zanzibar by 1885

▨ Areas already under Portuguese control in 1875

══1891══ Colonial frontiers with date of fixing

······ Frontiers of Congo Free State, as laid down by Berlin Conference in 1885

▓ Lado Enclave

→ Main routes of British advance during the Partition

→ Main routes of French advance during the Partition

-→ Main routes of German advance during the Partition

-→ Main routes of Portuguese advance during the Partition

--→ Main routes of Congo Free State (Leopold II) advance during the Partition

Main areas occupied by the colonial powers
Britain
Bechuanaland
British Central Africa (later Nyasaland)
British East Africa (Kenya)
Rhodesia
Uganda
Zanzibar

France
Chad
Gabon
Madagascar
Middle Congo
Ubangi Chari

Germany
German East Africa
Kamerun
South-West Africa

Congo Free State (founded by Leopold II of Belgium, 1885; taken over by Belgium, 1908)
Lado Enclave

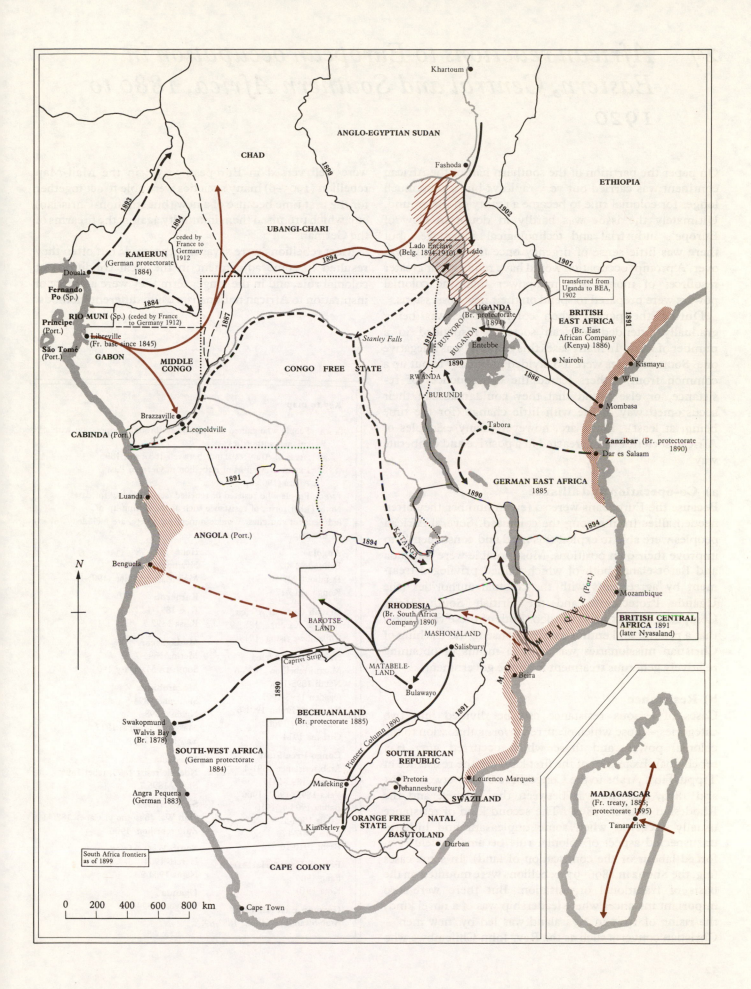

27 African reactions to European occupation in Eastern, Central and Southern Africa, 1880 to 1920

On paper the partition of the southern half of the African continent was carried out very rapidly; but it took much longer for colonial rule to become a reality on the ground. Ultimately the issue was hardly in doubt in view of Europe's industrial and technological advantages, but there was little sense of urgency once the Scramble was over. A prompt occupation would have required far greater resources of money and manpower than the colonial powers were prepared to spend on their new possessions.

During the period when colonial rule was being gradually extended, African societies responded in a number of ways. In many cases this response was a negative one. Some societies were too divided politically to put up a common front. Others feared the consequences of resistance, or else found that they could maintain their accustomed way of life with little change (for the time being, at least). There are, however, many examples of African societies which reacted in a positive and deliberate way.

a) Co-operation and alliance

Because the Europeans were so few in number they often needed allies from among the colonised. Several African peoples were able to exploit this need and consequently to improve their own positions. Most notable were Buganda and Barotseland, both of which gained privileged treatment by agreements with the colonial authorities (the Uganda Protectorate and the British South Africa Company, respectively) in 1900. Both of these cases show that a prompt and enthusiastic response to the teaching of Christian missionaries was often a means of obtaining relatively generous treatment from the government.

b) Resistance

Cases of serious resistance can be divided into two categories – those which occurred *before* submission to the colonial power, and those which occurred *after* (i.e. rebellions). Examples of the first kind are the resistance of Tippu Tib's Arabs to the Congo Free State between 1891 and 1894, and the war between the Ndebele and the Rhodesian settlers (1893). The second kind of resistance usually occurred when some unpleasant and hitherto unsuspected aspect of colonial rule became evident (e.g. forced labour or the confiscation of land). In some cases (e.g. the Shona in 1896–97) rebellions were mounted on the basis of traditional organisation. But there were also important instances where leadership was of a novel kind: the rising of 1915 in Nyasaland was led by 'new men' – Christian converts such as the Rev. John Chilembwe who

were well versed in European ways; in the Maji-Maji rebellion (1905–6) many societies were able to act together for the first time because of a new (but still non-Christian) cult which promised them immunity against the firearms of the Germans.

Most rebellions were savagely repressed; but often they resulted in some adjustment in the local conditions of colonial rule, and in the longer term they were a source of inspiration to African nationalists using different methods.

Key to map

CEWA People who gained conspicuously through cooperation with colonial authorities

▨ Areas of Arab resistance between 1887 and 1895

▧ Extent of Maji-Maji Rebellion in German East Africa (1905-6)

EMBU People who resisted or rebelled (see list below for dates)
Note: Other forms of resistance such as the setting up of independent churches, Wankie miners' strike etc. are included on the map.

Angola
Bailundo 1902
Dembos 1907-10
Kongo 1913-17

British Central Africa
Arabs of Karonga 1887-95
Chilembwe rising 1915

British East Africa
Mazrui rebellion 1895-6
Nandi 1895-1906
Ogaden 1898-1901
Kikuyu & Embu 1901-6
Gusii 1905, 1908
Giriama 1914

Congo Free State
Arab resistance 1891-4
Azande 1892-1917
Yaka 1895, 1902, 1906
Babua 1903-4, 1910
Budja 1903-5
Luba 1907-17
Bashi 1910-16

French Equatorial Africa
Fang 1906
Kota 1910

German East Africa
Arab-Swahili rebellion 1883-89,

Hehe 1891-98
Nyamwezi 1892-3
Maji-Maji rebellion 1905-6

Kamerun
Kpe 1891-4
Bassa 1892-5

Madagascar
Merina 1895-7
Southern Malagasy 1904-5

Mozambique
Shangane 1894-5
Ngoni 1898
Makombe (Shona) 1917
Yao 1900-12

Rhodesia
Ndebele resist 1893, rebel 1896
Shona 1896-7

South Africa
Gun War (Basotho v. Cape) 1880-1
Zulu rebellion 1906

South-West Africa
Herero 1904
Nama 1904-9

Uganda
Bunyoro 1894-7

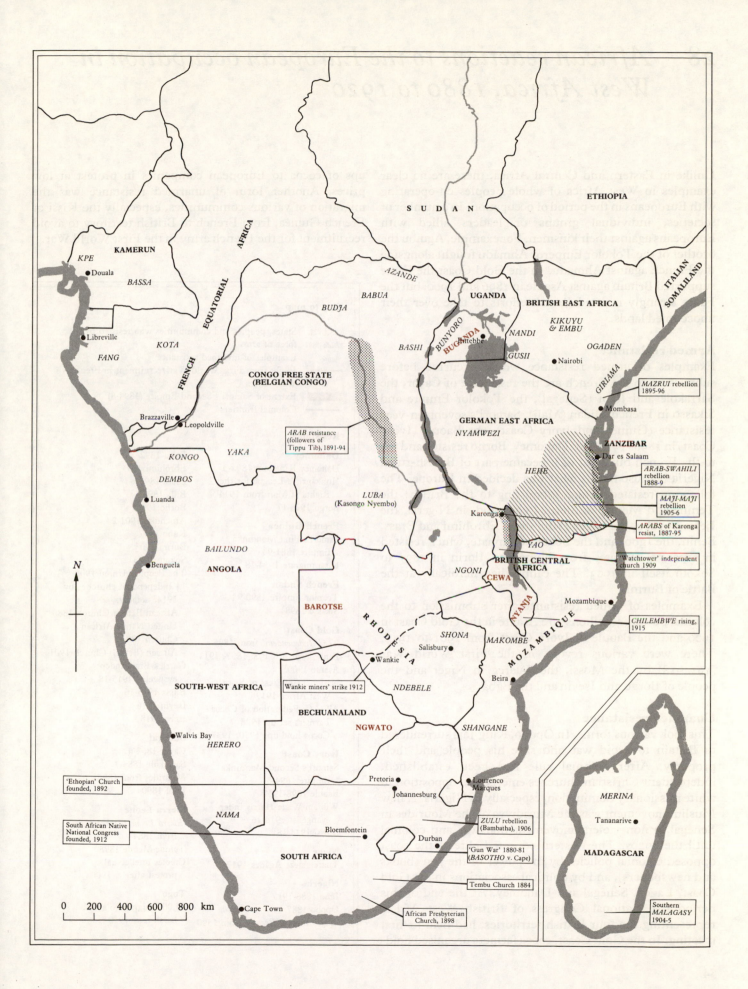

KAMERUN

KPE
● Douala

BASSA

FRENCH EQUATORIAL AFRICA

AZANDE

SUDAN

ETHIOPIA

ITALIAN SOMALILAND

● Libreville

FANG

KOTA

BABUA

BUDJA

UGANDA

BRITISH EAST AFRICA

BASHI
BUNYORO
BUGANDA ● Entebbe

NANDI

KIKUYU & EMBU

OGADEN

GUSII

GIRIAMA

● Nairobi

CONGO FREE STATE (BELGIAN CONGO)

YAKA

ARAB resistance (followers of Tippu Tib), 1891-94

MAZRUI rebellion 1895-96

● Mombasa

GERMAN EAST AFRICA

NYAMWEZI

ZANZIBAR

● Dar es Salaam

● Brazzaville
● Leopoldville

KONGO

DEMBOS

LUBA (Kasongo Nyembo)

HEHE

ARAB-SWAHILI rebellion 1888-9

MAJI-MAJI rebellion 1905-6

● Luanda

BAILUNDO

ARABS of Karonga resist, 1887-95

● Karonga

YAO

'Watchtower' independent church 1909

ANGOLA

● Benguela

N

BAROTSE

NGONI

CEWA

BRITISH CENTRAL AFRICA

NYANJA

● Mozambique

CHILEMBWE rising, 1915

R H O D E S I A

SHONA

MAKOMBE

MOZAMBIQUE

● Salisbury

● Wankie

NDEBELE

● Beira

Wankie miners' strike 1912

SOUTH-WEST AFRICA

BECHUANALAND

NGWATO

SHANGANE

● Walvis Bay

HERERO

'Ethopian' Church founded, 1892

MERINA

● Tananarive

South African Native National Congress founded, 1912

NAMA

● Pretoria

● Johannesburg

● Bloemfontein

● Lourenço Marques

ZULU rebellion (Bambatha), 1906

● Durban

'Gun War' 1880-81 (*BASOTHO* v. Cape)

MADAGASCAR

SOUTH AFRICA

Tembu Church 1884

0 200 400 600 800 km

● Cape Town

African Presbyterian Church, 1898

Southern *MALAGASY* 1904-5

African reactions to the European occupation in West Africa, 1880 to 1920

Unlike in Eastern and Central Africa, there are no clear examples in West Africa of whole peoples co-operating with Europeans in the period of occupation. In a number of societies, individual groups or leaders allied with Europeans against their kinsmen. For example, Aguibu the brother of the Tokolor Emperor Ahmadu fought alongside the French against Ahmadu. In the Gold Coast the Fante supported Britain against Asante in 1896 and 1900, but the Fante strongly resisted British efforts to take over their unoccupied lands.

Armed resistance

Examples of armed resistance which occurred before submission to the French are the resistance of Cayor, the Sarrakole and Jolof (Senegal), the Tokolor Empire and Sikasso in French Sudan (Mali), Samori's seventeen-year resistance (Guinea and Ivory Coast), the Baoule (Ivory Coast) in 1898–1917, and Dahomey. Borno resisted and fell to the French but most of it became part of British-ruled Nigeria because that is what was decided in Europe. The following resisted before submitting to the British: the Temne and Mende in Sierra Leone and, in Nigeria, the Ijebu Yoruba, the Niger Delta states Ebrohimi and Brass, Benin, the Igbo, and the Sokoto Caliphate, which resisted in separate emirates from Nupe and Ilorin in 1897 to Sokoto itself in 1903. The caliph died heroically at the Battle of Burmi.

Examples of armed resistance after submission to the colonial power (rebellions) are Asante in the Gold Coast in 1900 and the Baoule in Ivory Coast from 1901 to 1917. There were various revolts in the First World War (1914–18) by the Mossi, the Tuareg in Niger and the people of Borgu and Iseyin and the Egba.

Unarmed resistance

This took various forms. In Opobo, King Jaja surrendered to Britain to avoid war and save his people and their property. After colonial rule had been established, independent Christian churches emerged in opposition to white missionary domination, especially in Nigeria. A new Muslim movement was the Muridiyya of the Mourides in Senegal, a non-violent movement that was anti-colonial until the 1920s. The western-educated elite of the coast opposed colonial policies by the power of the pen (books and newspapers), and by political associations in the Gold Coast, Lagos, Senegal and Dahomey. At the end of this period the National Congress of British West Africa, representing the four British territories, had held its first meeting. In the Gold Coast, cocoa farmers organised hold-ups of cocoa to European companies in protest at low prices. Another form of unarmed resistance was the migration of various communities, especially the Kissi of French Guinea, from French to British territory to avoid recruitment for the French army in the First World War.

Key to map

ASANTE **Bida** 1897	States, peoples and communities who resisted by force of arms
Fante	Examples of unarmed resistance
→	Flight from First World War recruitment in French West Africa
▬	Extent of Samori's Second Empire (1894-8)
──	Colonial frontiers

Resistance

Dahomey
Dahomey Kingdom 1892-3
Hunkanrin's League for the
  Rights of Man from 1914
Borgu 1916-17

French Guinea
Samori's First Mandinka
  Empire 1881-94
Kissi migrate 1914-18

French Sudan
Tokolor Empire 1890-94
Sikasso 1898

Gold Coast
'G.C. Independent' from 1895
Fante form A.R.P.S. 1897, 1911
Asante 1900
National Congress of British
  West Africa 1919
All G.C. Federation of Cocoa
  Farmers set up 1928
Cocoa hold-ups 1930, 1937

Ivory Coast
Samori's Second Mandinka
  Empire 1894-8
Baoule 1898-1917
William Wade Harris indep.
  evangelist 1914-16
Mossi 1914-18

Niger
Tuareg sieze Agades 1917

Nigeria
Igbo 1886-1917
Opobo 1887
'*Lagos Weekly Record*' from 1890

Ijebu 1892
Ebrohimi 1894
Brass 1895
Bida 1897
Borno 1900
Arochuku 1901-2
Kano 1902
Burmi 1903
Sokoto 1903
The People's Union 1908
14 Independent churches by
  1914, notably:
  African Baptist Church 1888
  United Native African
    Church 1891
  African (Bethel) Church 1901
Garrick Braid indep.
  evangelist 1915-18
Bussa 1915-16
Iseyin 1916
Egba 1918

Senegal
Cayor 1883-6
Sarrakole 1885-7
Mourides from 1886
Jolof 1890

Sierra Leone
'*Sierra Leone Weekly News*'
  from 1884
Temne-Mende 1898
Creoles intellectual
  protest after c. 1900

Togo
14,000 migrate to avoid
  harsh laws 1910

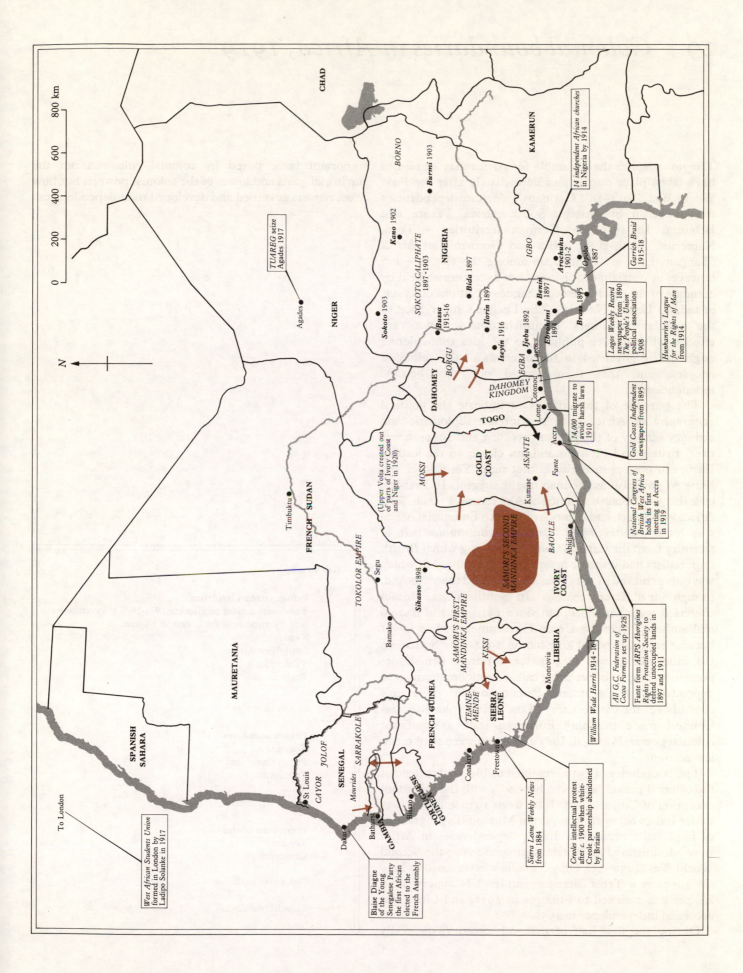

CHAD

KAMERUN

BORNO

Burmi 1903

Kano 1902

NIGERIA

IGBO

14 independent African churches
in Nigeria by 1914

Arochuku
1901-2

Opobo
1887

Garrick Braid
1915-18

Sokoto 1903

SOKOTO CALIPHATE
1897–1903

Bida 1897

Benin
1897

Brass 1895

Lagos Weekly Record
newspaper from 1890
The People's Union
political association
1908

TUAREG seize
Agades 1917

NIGER

Ilorin 1897

Ebrohimi
1894

Hunkanrin's League
for the Rights of Man
from 1914

Agades

Bussa
1915-16

Iseyin 1916

Ijebu 1892

EGBA Lagos

14,000 migrate to
avoid harsh laws
1910

BORGU

DAHOMEY

Cotonou

DAHOMEY
KINGDOM

Lome

TOGO

Gold Coast Independent
newspaper from 1895

(Upper Volta created out
of parts of Ivory Coast
and Niger in 1920)

MOSSI

GOLD
COAST

Accra

National Congress of
British West Africa
holds its first
meeting at Accra
in 1919

FRENCH SUDAN

Timbuktu

ASANTE

Kumase

Fante

BAOULE

SAMORI'S SECOND
MANDINKA EMPIRE

IVORY
COAST

Abidjan

All G.C. Federation of
Cocoa Farmers set up 1928

Segu

TOKOLOR EMPIRE

Sikasso 1898

LIBERIA

KISSI

Fante form ARPS Aborigines
Rights Protection Society to
defend unoccupied lands in
1897 and 1911

MAURETANIA

Bamako

SAMORI'S FIRST
MANDINKA EMPIRE

TEMNE
MENDE

SIERRA
LEONE

Monrovia

William Wade Harris 1914–16

Conakry

FRENCH GUINEA

Freetown

Creoles intellectual protest
after c. 1900 when white–
Creole partnership abandoned
by Britain

SPANISH
SAHARA

CAYOR *JOLOF*

SENEGAL *SARRAKOLE*

Sierra Leone Weekly News
from 1884

St Louis

Mourides

PORTUGUESE
GUINEA

Bissao

To London

Dakar

Bathurst

GAMBIA

West African Students Union
formed in London by
Ladipo Solanke in 1917

Blaise Diagne of the Young
Senegalese Party
the first African
elected to the
French Assembly

N

800 km

600

400

200

0

The last stage in the Scramble for Africa may be said to have taken place during and immediately after the First World War (1914–18). Germany's African dependencies were overrun by Britain, South Africa, France and Belgium. In 1919 the German territories – Togo, Kamerun, South-West Africa and German East Africa (Tanganyika) were divided up among the victors – not however as outright acquisitions but as territories held by mandate of the newly created League of Nations (ancestor of today's United Nations). The League's supervision of the mandatory powers' administration was not very effective, but it gave publicity to the idea that colonies ought to be governed in the interests of the colonised peoples, and that these would one day become independent.

The purpose of this map is to indicate the political geography of Africa once the intense diplomatic and military activity of the years 1875–1903 and 1914–19 was over. Britain and France stand out clearly as the leading European powers in Africa at that time. Yet neither was quite so powerful as the map might suggest. In France's case this was because so much of Algeria and French West Africa was desert, and so much of French Equatorial Africa was totally undeveloped. Britain's continuous belt of territory from the Cape to Cairo (something which British imperialists had set their hearts on in the 1880s but which was only achieved in 1919) was also less solid than it looked, though for different reasons. In South Africa, Britain exercised some influence, but since 1910 she had had no real authority over the Union Government, while Egypt became an independent kingdom in 1922. The Sudan, on the other hand, was in practice a purely British dependency, in spite of her being called a condominium (i.e. a dependency of Egypt and Britain jointly). Belgium's control over the vast territory of the Congo (plus Ruanda-Urundi) made this tiny European state a significant colonial power. Portugal, Italy and Spain were all of much less account.

The boundaries of 1919 remained stable until the end of the colonial period (and even beyond), with the important exception of Ethiopia, which between 1936 and 1941 was under Italian occupation as part of Mussolini's programme of imperialist expansion. Italy's dependencies in Africa were administered by Britain during and after the Second World War (1939–45). Only Somalia was returned to Italy (in 1950, as a Trust Territory under UN supervision). Eritrea was annexed to Ethiopia in 1952, and Libya was accorded independence in 1951.

During the first half of the 20th century, the really important issue posed by colonial rule was not the territorial gains and losses of the colonial powers, but how those powers governed and developed their dependencies.

Key to map

〰〰〰 Former German territories.
These were divided up after the 1914-18 War as territories held by mandate of the League of Nations:
Kamerun
South-West Africa
Tanganyika
Togoland

//// British territories

British mandates
Togoland
British Cameroons
Tanganyika

▨▨▨ French territories

French mandates
Togoland
Cameroun

//// Portuguese territories

——— Colonial boundaries

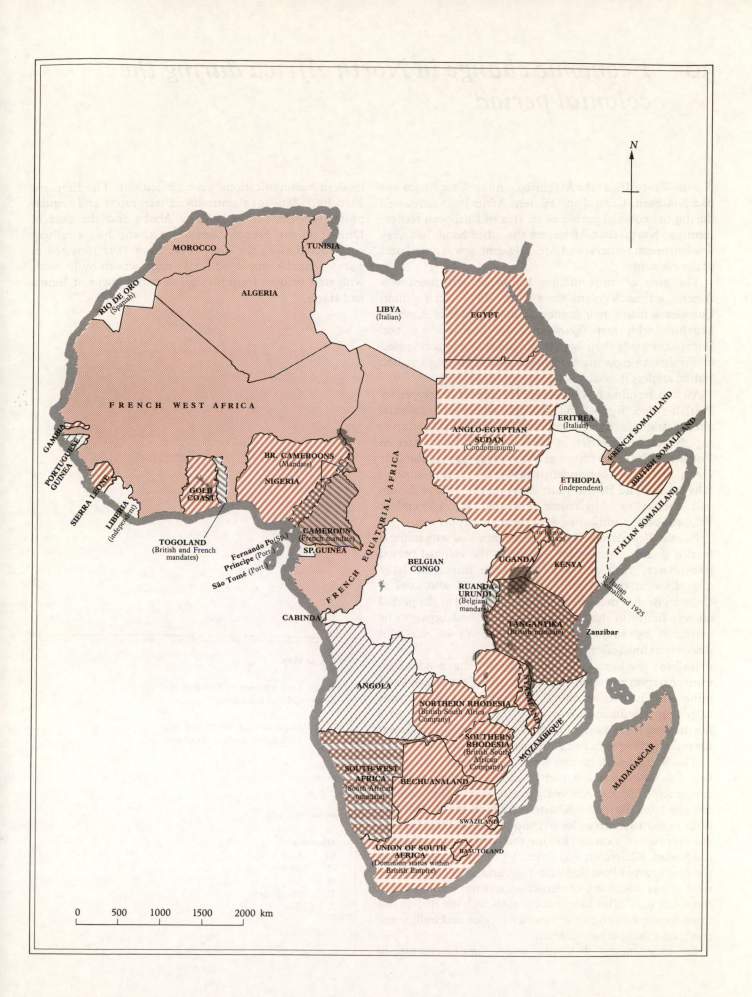

MOROCCO

TUNISIA

RIO DE ORO
(Spanish)

ALGERIA

LIBYA
(Italian)

EGYPT

GAMBIA

PORTUGUESE
GUINEA

SIERRA LEONE

LIBERIA
(independent)

FRENCH WEST AFRICA

ANGLO-EGYPTIAN
SUDAN
(Condominium)

ERITREA
(Italian)

FRENCH SOMALILAND

BRITISH SOMALILAND

GOLD
COAST

BR. CAMEROONS
(Mandate)

NIGERIA

ETHIOPIA
(independent)

ITALIAN SOMALILAND

TOGOLAND
(British and French
mandates)

Fernando Po (Sp.)
Príncipe (Port.)
São Tomé (Port.)

CAMEROUN
(French mandate)

SP. GUINEA

FRENCH EQUATORIAL AFRICA

to Kenya
1926

UGANDA

KENYA

BELGIAN
CONGO

RUANDA-
URUNDI
(Belgian)
mandate)

to Italian
Somaliland 1925

CABINDA

TANGANYIKA
(British mandate)

Zanzibar

ANGOLA

NORTHERN RHODESIA
(British South Africa
Company)

SOUTHERN
RHODESIA
(British South
African Company)

MOZAMBIQUE

MADAGASCAR

SOUTH-WEST
AFRICA
(South African
mandate)

BECHUANALAND

SWAZILAND

UNION OF SOUTH
AFRICA
(Dominion status within
British Empire)

BASUTOLAND

N

0   500   1000   1500   2000 km

30 Economic change in North Africa during the colonial period

North-West Africa (the Maghrib), unlike West Africa but like Southern, Central and Eastern Africa, was developed during the colonial period as an area of European settler-farming. North-East Africa, on the other hand, had very few European settlers, and African farming was a vital part of the economy.

The area of most intense European settlement was Algeria, a French colony since 1830, where over a million Europeans made their homes, at the expense of Algerian Muslims who lost their land. In Morocco 550,000 Europeans made their homes and another 250,000 settled in Tunisia, to grow mainly wine or wheat. In Libya 70,000 Italian settlers moved in.

African farming of cash crops for export developed in British-ruled Egypt and Sudan, where the colonial administration actively encouraged production of cotton to supply textile factories in the county of Lancashire in England. The main cotton growing areas were in the Nile Delta and in the government-run Gezira scheme south of Khartoum. The British built dams on the Nile at Aswan and Sennar to help cotton growing. In independent Ethiopia cotton and coffee were the main export crops.

North-West Africa is much better endowed with mineral wealth than is North-East Africa. In the colonial period phosphates, zinc and iron ore were mined in large quantities in the Maghrib countries, and also coal at Colomb Bechar in Algeria. Towards the end of the period oil was found in the Sahara in Algeria, and began to be extracted by French companies. Libya's oil was not discovered until after independence.

Railway building was essential for the production, transportation and export of North Africa's cash crops and minerals. The densest railway networks were in the major cash crop producing areas of lower Egypt and Algeria north of the Atlas mountains. Railways were also important for military purposes and administration.

The Sudan, with its vast size and scattered population, began to be knotted together by the new railway network constructed under Anglo-Egyptian rule. The military railway from Egypt to Khartoum which the British had built in the 1890s in order to conquer the country became the first part of a system linking the northern provinces of the Sudan. Khartoum was linked by rail to the Red Sea at the new town of Port Sudan in 1905 and to El Obeid in the west in 1911. Railway construction was not undertaken in the south until after independence, though the British did improve the existing river steamer service and built some roads into the southern Sudan.

In independent Ethiopia major improvements in modern communications were carried out. The Emperor Menelik (1889–1913) introduced telegraphs and regular postal services between Addis Ababa and the port of Djibuti on the French Somali coast, and had a railway constructed along the same route from 1892 (finished in 1915). Menelik employed Swiss engineers to build roads with steel bridges from his capital to the towns of Jimma and Harar.

Key to map

///// Land occupied by European settlers

——— Colonial boundaries

▓▓▓ Major areas of African cash crop
COFFEE Agricultural produce for export
COTTON
SUGAR
WHEAT
WINE

▬▭▬ Railways

Minerals
Cl Coal
Ir Iron ore
O Oil
P Phosphates
Z Zinc

⌁⌁⌁ Sudd

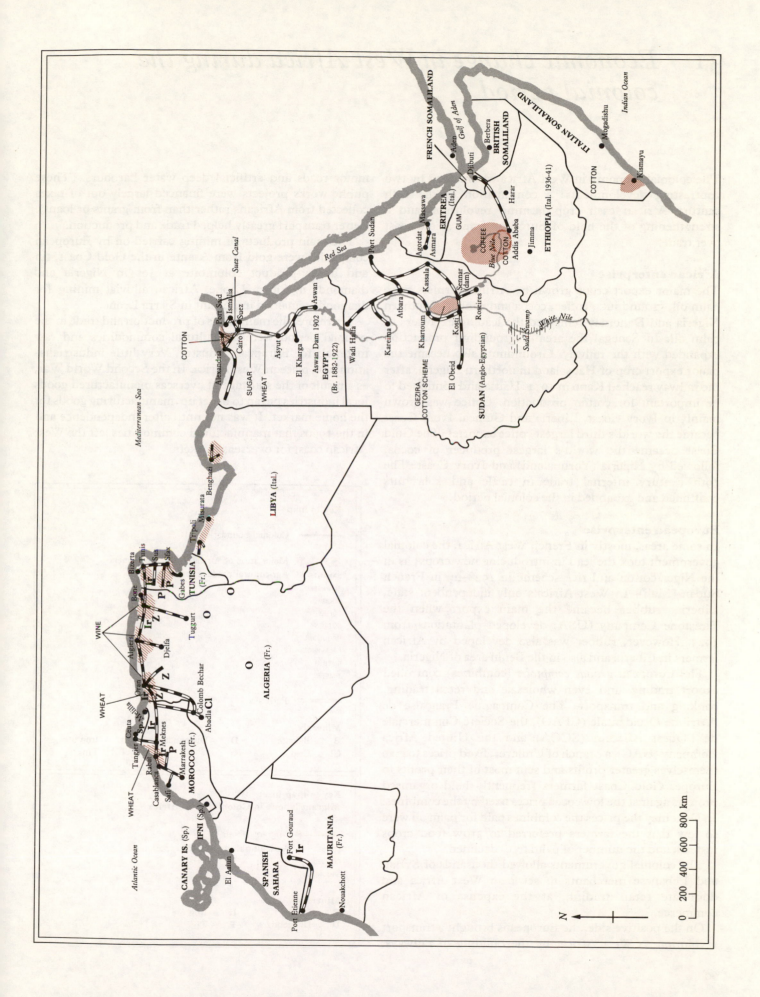

31 Economic change in West Africa during the colonial period

The colonial economy in West Africa was marked by two contrasting developments: a continuation of the 19th century African cash crop farming revolution, and a strengthening of the hold of European firms at the coast over trade.

African enterprise

The major export crops grown by African farmers were palm oil, groundnuts, coffee, cocoa and rubber. Southern Nigeria and Dahomey remained the leading exporters of palm oil. In Senegal the area of groundnut production expanded with the railway. Groundnuts also became the major export crop of Hausaland in northern Nigeria, after the railway reached Kano in 1911. Hausaland continued to be important for cotton production. Coffee was grown mainly in Ivory Coast, Liberia and Guinea. Ivory Coast became the world's third largest coffee exporter. The Gold Coast became the world's largest producer of cocoa, followed by Nigeria (Yorubaland) and Ivory Coast. The 19th century internal trade in cattle and kola nuts continued and expanded in the colonial period.

European enterprise

In some areas, mostly in French West Africa, the colonial government took the lead in introducing new crops; as in the Niger cotton and rice scheme in 1928–29 in French Sudan (Mali). In West Africa's only independent state, Liberia, rubber became the main export when the Firestone Company (USA) developed plantations from 1925. However, rubber was also developed by African farmers in Liberia and also in the Benin area of Nigeria.

The European *grands comptoirs* (combines) controlled export trading, and even wholesale and retail trading, banking and transport. The Compagnie Française de l'Afrique Occidentale (CFAO), the Société Commerciale de l'Ouest Africain (SCOA) and the United Africa Company (UAC), a branch of Unilever, fixed prices to give themselves greater profits and sent most of their profits to Europe. Gold Coast farmers frequently held organised protests against the low cocoa prices fixed by the combines. In Dahomey the prices the combines paid for palm oil were so low that the farmers preferred to grow food crops instead, and the number of palm trees declined.

The colonial governments allowed thousands of Syrian and Lebanese merchants to settle in West Africa and dominate retail trading, at the expense of African commerce.

On the positive side, the Europeans brought a transport revolution to West Africa, by the building of railways, motor roads and artificial deep-water harbours. (These public works projects were financed largely out of taxes collected from Africans rather than from grants or loans). Better transport greatly helped trade and production.

The main products of mining carried on by European companies were gold from Asante in the Gold Coast, tin and its by-product columbite at Jos in Nigeria and diamonds in Sierra Leone. African alluvial mining for diamonds remained important in Sierra Leone.

Therefore, the main items of production and trade in the colonial period were agricultural commodities and raw materials for European industry. Very little industrialisation took place in West Africa. In the Second World War, as a result of the shortage of overseas manufactured goods local industries began to be set up, manufacturing goods for the home market. It was not until after independence and in the 1960s that manufactured commodities left the West African coast for overseas markets.

Key to map

——— Colonial boundaries

▨ Major areas of African cash crop farmers

BANANAS   Agricultural produce for export
BENNISEED
COCOA
COFFEE
COTTON
GROUNDNUTS
PALM PRODUCTS
RUBBER
TIMBER

▬▭▬ Railways

Minerals

B	Bauxite	D	Diamonds	Ir	Iron ore
Cl	Coal	G	Gold	T	Tin

Key to map inset
Migrant labour in Colonial West Africa

⟶ Migrant labour

COCOA   Agricultural produce for export
COFFEE
GROUNDNUTS

Minerals

C	Coal	Ir	Iron ore
D	Diamonds	T	Tin

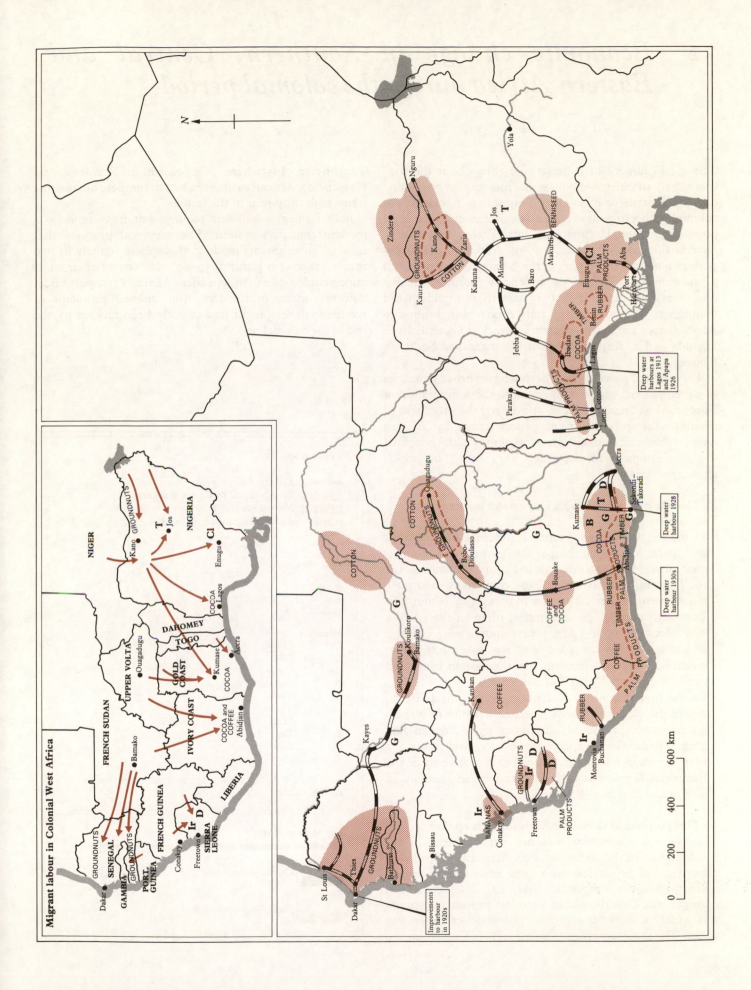

Migrant labour in Colonial West Africa

NIGER

GROUNDNUTS

Kano

T

Jos NIGERIA

Cl

Enugu

COCOA

Lagos

DAHOMEY

TOGO

Ouagadugu

UPPER VOLTA

GOLD COAST

Kumase COCOA

Accra

IVORY COAST COCOA and COFFEE

Abidjan

LIBERIA

FRENCH SUDAN

SENEGAL

Bamako

FRENCH GUINEA

Ir D

Conakry Freetown SIERRA LEONE

GROUNDNUTS

GAMBIA

PORT. GUINEA

Dakar

Nguru

Zinder

Kano

Kaura

Zaria

GROUNDNUTS

COTTON

Jos T

Yola

BENNISEED

Kaduna

Minna

Baro

Makurdi

Cl

PALM PRODUCTS

Benin RUBBER

Enugu

Port Aba Harcourt

Jebba

Ibadan COCOA

Lagos

PALM PRODUCTS

Cotonou

Lomé

Parakou

Accra

Deep water harbours at Lagos 1913 and Apapa 1926

Ouagadugu

COTTON

GROUNDNUTS

Bobo-Dioulasso

COTTON

G

Koulikoro

Bamako

GROUNDNUTS

G

Kayes

Kankan

COFFEE

Kumase

COCOA

B

G T D

G Sekundi-Takoradi

TIMBER

Bouake

RUBBER

COFFEE and COCOA

Abidjan

PALM PRODUCTS

COFFEE

TIMBER

RUBBER

Deep water harbour 1928

Deep water harbour 1930s

Ir

RUBBER

Monrovia

Buchanan

St Louis

Thies

Bathurst

GROUNDNUTS

Bissau

Ir

BANANAS

Conakry

Ir D

GROUNDNUTS

Freetown

PALM PRODUCTS

D

PALM PRODUCTS

Improvements to harbour in 1920s

0   200   400   600 km

32 Economic change in Southern, Central and Eastern Africa during the colonial period

The establishment of colonial rule throughout the southern half of Africa made some measure of economic development there inevitable. This was not because the colonial authorities desired the advancement of the local population (though some did), but because they had to recover the costs of administration. Initially none of the powers who had taken part in the Scramble was prepared to subsidise its African dependencies for more than a few years. Not until after 1945 was there a widespread willingness to channel large state funds from Europe to Africa (hence the hydro-electric schemes at Owen Falls in Uganda and at Kariba, between Northern and Southern Rhodesia).

The colonial powers chose between two broad strategies of development: one was to promote the immigration of Europeans as farmers and businessmen; the other was to promote the production of export crops by African farmers. How far economic development actually benefited the local population depended very much on which strategy was adopted.

a) Development through European enterprise

This took two forms.

1 In the Belgian Congo, French Equatorial Africa (AEF) and parts of Mozambique the government granted control over land and minerals to European companies in the form of 'concessions'. These companies used their government-conferred powers to press local labour into European plantations and mines, often in the crudest way. Between 1908–14 the worst abuses were checked and much of the conceded land was taken into direct control by the government, but the system continued until the Second World War (see inset).

2 In the highland areas of Eastern and Central Africa, where the climate allowed permanent white residence, governments promoted settlement by European farmers. Africans were expected to provide farm labour at a very low wage, and the growing of cash crops outside the European farms was actively discouraged (notably in Kenya and Southern Rhodesia).

b) Development through African enterprise

This second alternative was not very evident in the southern half of the continent. Few Africans had previous experience of producing on a large scale for the export market, unlike in West Africa (Map 17). The outstanding example was Uganda, where a modest peasant prosperity was widely shared through the cultivation of cotton and coffee. The same was true of limited areas of Cameroun and

Tanganyika. Elsewhere (e.g. Northern Rhodesia and Nyasaland), African cash crops had to compete on unequal terms with the power of the settlers.

Both strategies had one requirement in common – a modern transport system. The very real progress that colonial governments made in this sphere (chiefly in two spurts: 1890–1914 and 1950–60) was one of their most important legacies to independent Africa. Transport aside, however, many of the most fundamental problems of economic development had scarcely been tackled by the end of the colonial period.

Key to map

- ▭▭▭ Railways
- ▨▨▨ Land occupied by European settlers
- ▨▨▨ Major areas of African cash crop farmers
- CLOVES   Agricultural produce for export
- COCOA
- COFFEE
- COTTON
- PALM PRODUCTS
- SISAL
- SUGAR
- TEA
- TOBACCO

Minerals

Ch	Chrome
Cl	Coal
Cp	Copper
D	Diamonds
G	Gold
Ir	Iron ore
L	Lead
T	Tin
U	Uranium
Z	Zinc

Note: For full details of South African, economic change see also Map 33.

Key to inset Map
Chartered companies and concessionaire companies

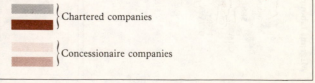

Chartered companies

Concessionaire companies

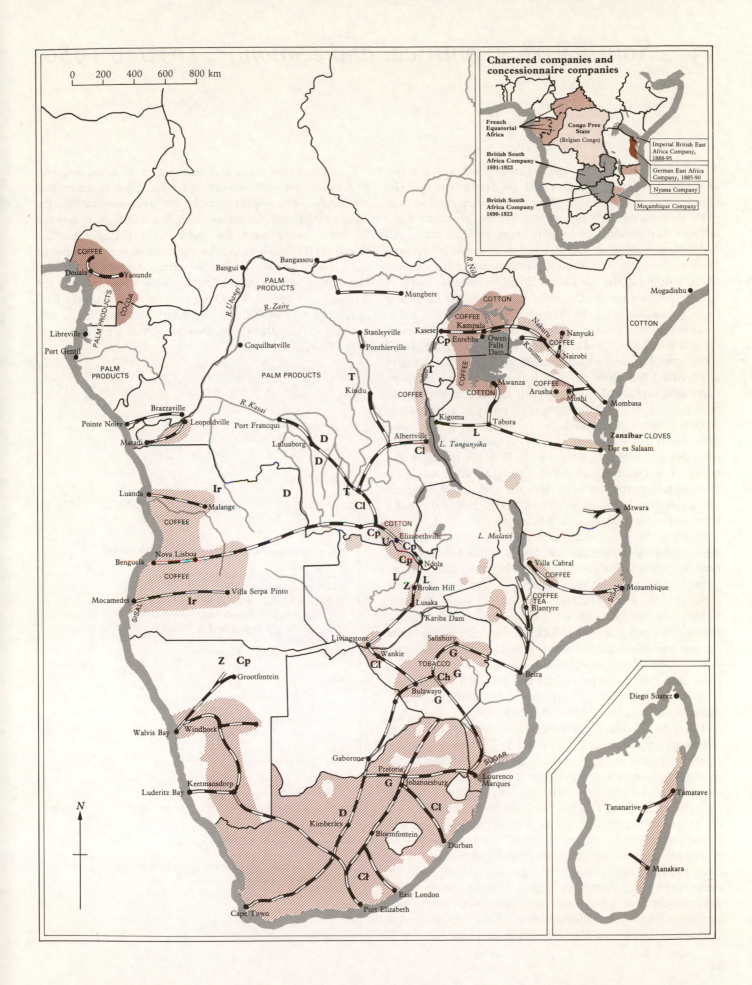

Chartered companies and concessionnaire companies

French Equatorial Africa

Congo Free State (Belgian Congo)

Imperial British East Africa Company, 1888-95

German East Africa Company, 1885-90

British South Africa Company 1891-1923

British South Africa Company 1890-1923

Nyassa Company

Moçambique Company

0 200 400 600 800 km

N

COFFEE
Douala
Yaounde
Bangui
Bangassou
PALM PRODUCTS
COCOA
Libreville
Port Gentil
PALM PRODUCTS
R. Ubangi
R. Zaire
Mungbere
COTTON
COFFEE
Kampala
Kasese
Entebbe
Owen Falls Dam
Nakuru
Nanyuki
COFFEE
Kisumu
Nairobi
Mogadishu
COTTON
Stanleyville
Ponthierville
Coquilhatville
PALM PRODUCTS
T
Kindu
COFFEE
T
COFFEE
COTTON
Mwanza
COFFEE
Arusha
Moshi
Mombasa
Brazzaville
R. Kasai
Port Francqui
Pointe Noire
Leopoldville
Matadi
Luluaborg
D
D
Albertville
Cl
Kigoma
Tabora
L
L. Tanganyika
Zanzibar CLOVES
Dar es Salaam
Ir
Luanda
Malange
D
T
Cl
Cp
COTTON
Elizabethville
Cp
Cp
Ndola
Mtwara
COFFEE
Nova Lisboa
Benguela
COFFEE
L. Malawi
Villa Cabral
COFFEE
Mozambique
Mocamedes
Ir
Villa Serpa Pinto
L
Z
Broken Hill
Lusaka
COFFEE
TEA
Blantyre
SISAL
Kariba Dam
Livingstone
Salisbury
G
Z Cp
Grootfontein
Wankie
Cl
TOBACCO
Ch G
Bulawayo
G
Beira
Diego Suarez
Walvis Bay
Windhoek
Gaborone
SUGAR
Tamatave
Tananarive
Keetmansdorp
Luderitz Bay
Pretoria
G
Johannesburg
Lourenco Marques
D
Kimberley
Cl
Manakara
Bloemfontein
Durban
Cl
East London
Cape Town
Port Elizabeth

The period since the creation of the Union has seen major changes in every sphere of life in South Africa. The country has become more intensively industrialised than ever. Compared with that of whites, the position of the African population has steadily worsened, as their civil rights have been whittled away and their wages held down. Within the white community, political power has become the monopoly of the Afrikaner (Boer) Nationalist Party. It has not hesitated to use the authority of the state ruthlessly to suppress dissidents, be they white or black.

The mines – gold (on the Witwatersrand), diamonds (round Kimberley) and coal (especially in northern Natal) – continued to be the backbone of South African industry after 1910; but from the 1930s manufacturing industry expanded rapidly also. As a result the urban population rose sharply too. By 1936 about one and a quarter million Africans were employed in the towns, but a high proportion of these were migrant workers, many of them from outside the Union (see inset). 'Poor whites' were also being drawn away from the countryside. Meanwhile on European farms the status of Africans declined from tenant farmer to wage labourer. Both in the country and the town, therefore, a black proletariat was emerging.

Despite the heavy dependence of industry on African labour, Africans were allowed only a trifling share of the benefits of industrialisation – wages (approximately 12 per cent of those of white workers), recreation facilities, medical care and education. South Africa's immense wealth was used to maintain the whites in a high standard of living at the expense of the black majority. By means of the colour bar (first placed on the statute book in 1911) Africans were kept out of skilled and well-paid jobs. Their total exclusion from provincial and national politics was only a matter of time: by 1956 the voting rights of the non-white population had been eliminated.

The first Union Government was led by Botha, an Afrikaner general from the Transvaal. Two turning points since then have confirmed the hold of the Afrikaners on government, and each brought about a hardening of attitude in racial matters. The first turning point was in 1924, when Hertzog and the National Party took office on the slogan of 'segregation'. The second turning point was in 1948 when Malan and the 'purified' Nationalists came to power pledged to a policy of 'apartheid' (separation). This party has enjoyed an overwhelming parliamentary majority since 1958 and shows no sign of losing power. The government was given sweeping powers to stamp out opposition under the Suppression of Communism Act (1950) and the Ninety-Day Detention Law (1963).

Confronted by such a concentration of economic and political power, African resistance has been sporadic and ineffective. The oldest African political association, the African National Congress (founded 1912), was banned in 1960, along with the more radical Pan-Africanist Congress (founded 1958). In 1963 the government began the creation of 'Bantustans' – semi-autonomous African homelands within South Africa – beginning with the Transkei. It hoped that this policy would not only lend apartheid respectability abroad but also provide a safe outlet for African frustrations at home. By 1980 these hopes had failed.

Key to map

South Africa, political and economic, 1910 to 1980

——— International boundaries
– – – Provincial boundaries
▨ Approximate extent of land held by Africans in South Africa (about 11% of total land in 1970)
▬ Railways
■ Main areas of industry

Minerals:
Cl Coal
Cp Copper
D Diamonds
G Gold
Ir Iron ore
M Manganese
T Tin
U Uranium

Key to inset map
Migrant labour in Southern Africa

▨ Main industrial areas employing migrant labour
——▶ Labour migration in existence by 1899
– –▶ 1914
——▶ 1925
– –▶ 1939

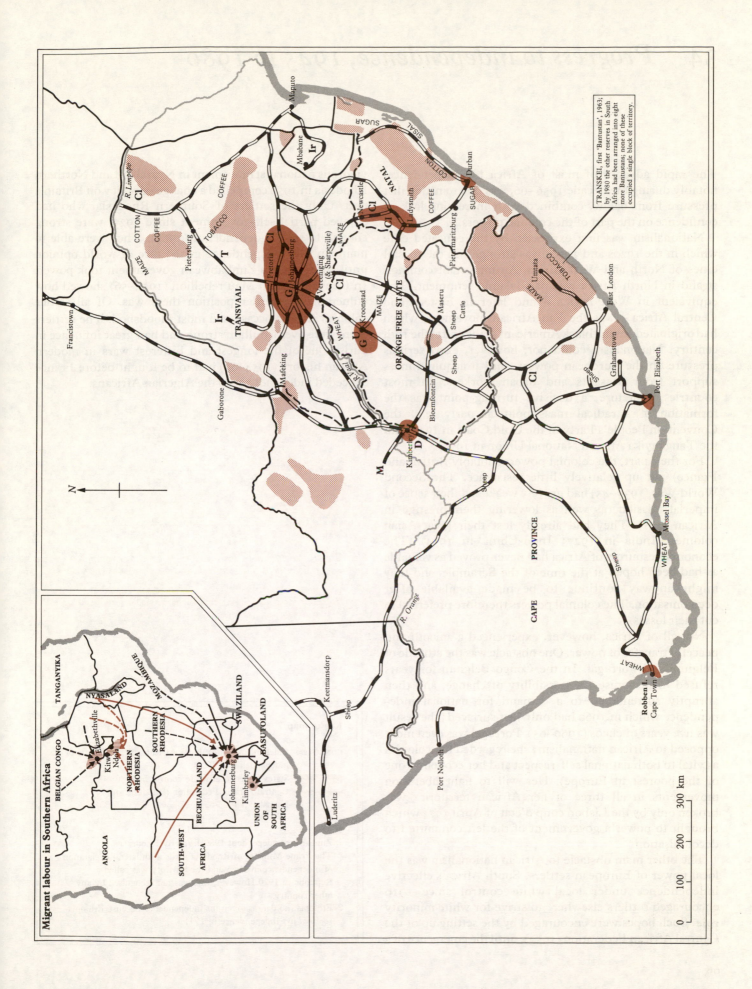

TRANSKEI, first 'Bantustan', 1963; by 1980 the other reserves in South Africa had been arranged into eight more Bantustans; none of these occupied a single block of territory.

Maputo

Mbabane **Ir**

Cl

R. Limpopo

COFFEE

COTTON

COFFEE

MAIZE

COFFEE

Pietersburg

TOBACCO

T

Cl

Pretoria

Johannesburg

G

Vereeniging (& Sharpeville)

Ir

TRANSVAAL

Mafeking

Cl

WHEAT

WHEAT

R. Vaal

Kroonstad

G U

Cl

ORANGE FREE STATE

MAIZE

Maseru

Sheep Cattle

Francistown

Gaborone

Bloemfontein

Sheep

Kimberley

D

M

Newcastle

Ladysmith

Cl

Cl

NATAL

Pietermaritzburg

COFFEE

Durban

SUGAR

SISAL

COTTON

SUGAR

Umtata

TOBACCO

MAIZE

East London

Grahamstown

Sheep

Cl

Cl

CAPE PROVINCE

Port Elizabeth

R. Orange

Sheep

Keetmansdorp

Sheep

Mossel Bay

WHEAT

WHEAT

Port Nolloth

Luderitz

Sheep

Robben I.
Cape Town

N

Migrant labour in Southern Africa

TANGANYIKA

BELGIAN CONGO

NYASALAND

Elizabethville

Kitwe Ndola

NORTHERN RHODESIA

MOZAMBIQUE

SOUTHERN RHODESIA

ANGOLA

SOUTH-WEST AFRICA

BECHUANALAND

SWAZILAND

BASUTOLAND

UNION OF SOUTH AFRICA

Johannesburg

Kimberley

300 km

200

100

0

The rapid advance of most of Africa to independence, notably during the decade 1956–66, was due to nationalist pressure from below, combined with increasing lack of confidence on the part of the colonial powers.

Nationalism was first expressed by the educated elite which in the 1920s and 1930s was strongest in the coastal cities of North and West Africa. An important common strand in North Africa was pan-Islamic sentiment. The equivalent in West Africa – and later in Eastern and Central Africa – was the Pan-African movement, which had originated among black Americans at the end of the 19th century. Nationalism could not, however, exert serious pressure on the European powers until it acquired mass support from peasants and urban workers. In most countries, therefore, a decisive turning-point was the formation of a radical mass political party (e.g. the Convention People's Party in the Gold Coast in 1949, and the Tanganyika African National Union in 1954).

For their part, the colonial powers (notably Britain and France) put up relatively little resistance. The Second World War (1939–45) had gravely weakened their sense of imperial mission (as well as lowering their prestige in African eyes). They had already lost their great Asian colonies (India in 1947; Indo-China in 1954). The economic resources of Africa had never proved as valuable as had been hoped at the time of the Scramble, and they might anyway continue to be made available after decolonisation. The colonial powers therefore preferred to cut their losses.

Not all of Africa, however, experienced a smooth and peaceful transfer of power. One obstacle was the attitude of Belgium and Portugal. In the Congo Belgium for years refused to recognise the possibility of change, and then abruptly surrendered to a demand for national independence which in 1960 had only just surfaced; the result was five years of chaos (1960–65). Portugal was even more opposed to African nationalism; she regarded her colonies as vital to both national self-respect and her economy (one of the poorest in Europe). Her will to fight liberation movements in all three of her African territories was broken only by the Lisbon coup d'état of April 1974 which brought to power a government of the left committed to decolonisation.

The other main obstacle to African nationalism was the local power of European settlers. South Africa's effective independence under local white control since 1910 encouraged settlers elsewhere to strive for white minority rule. Such hopes were encouraged by the setting up of the Central African Federation (1953), until the emergence of a vigorous nationalist movement in Nyasaland and Northern Rhodesia in 1959 compelled a change of policy on Britain's part. Only the settlers of Southern Rhodesia, who had enjoyed partial self-government since 1923, were strong enough to seize independence (1965). They were able to maintain this independence in the face of world opinion until 1980, when a Zimbabwean government took power. In Kenya the Mau Mau rebellion (1952–56) showed how vulnerable the settler position there was. Of all settler colonies Algeria occasioned most bloodshed. The settlers there were over a million strong and had great influence in Paris. One of the longest and bitterest wars in modern African history (1954–62) had to be fought before France conceded independence to the Algerian Africans.

Key to map

CONGO 1960 Independent states under African rule, with date of independence

States under local white control in 1980

——— Central African Federation (Rhodesia and Nyasaland) 1953-63

Notes

1 Zimbabwe: (independent 1980) formerly Rhodesia.
   The Prime Minister of Rhodesia made a unilateral declaration of independence in 1965 and the territory was called a Republic in 1970. However, this was not recognised by any other country.
2 Ethiopia: no date is given for independence because Ethiopia *regained* her independence in 1941.

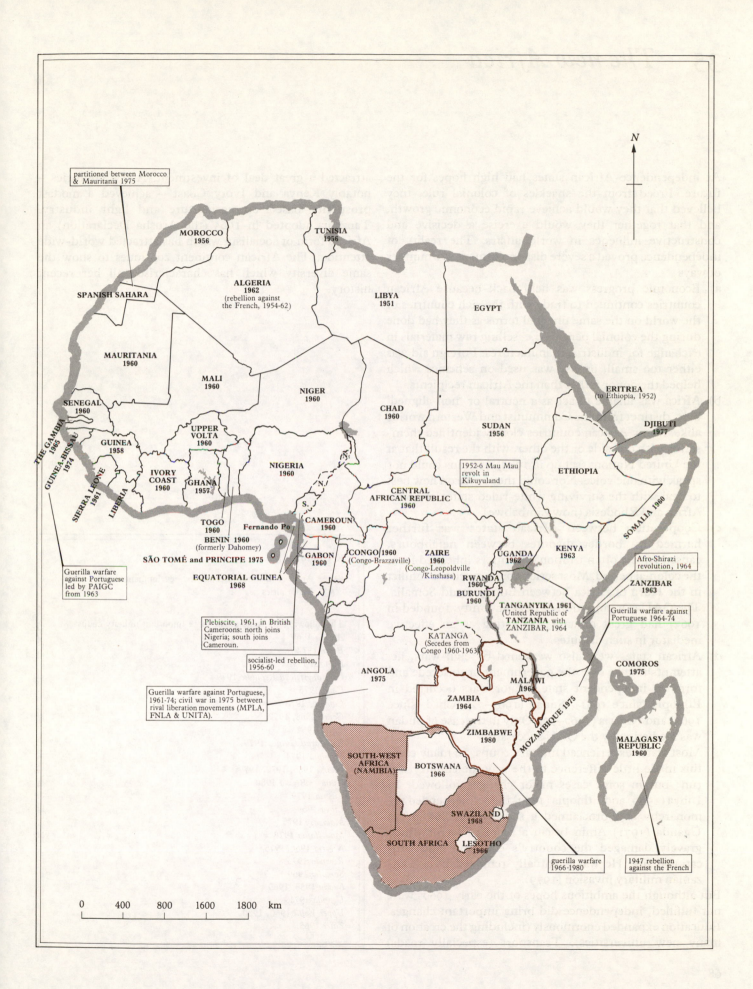

N

partitioned between Morocco
& Mauritania 1975

MOROCCO
1956

TUNISIA
1956

SPANISH SAHARA

ALGERIA
1962
(rebellion against
the French, 1954-62)

LIBYA
1951

EGYPT

MAURITANIA
1960

MALI
1960

NIGER
1960

CHAD
1960

SUDAN
1956

ERITREA
(to Ethiopia, 1952)

DJIBUTI
1977

SENEGAL
1960

THE GAMBIA
1965

GUINEA-BISSAU
1974

GUINEA
1958

SIERRA LEONE
1961

LIBERIA

IVORY
COAST
1960

UPPER
VOLTA
1960

GHANA
1957

NIGERIA
1960

N.

1952-6 Mau Mau
revolt in
Kikuyuland

ETHIOPIA

SOMALIA 1960

Guerilla warfare
against Portuguese
led by PAIGC
from 1963

TOGO
1960

BENIN 1960
(formerly Dahomey)

Fernando Po

CAMEROUN
1960

CENTRAL
AFRICAN REPUBLIC
1960

SÃO TOMÉ and PRINCIPE 1975

GABON
1960

CONGO 1960
(Congo-Brazzaville)

ZAIRE
1960
(Congo-Leopoldville
/Kinshasa)

UGANDA
1962

KENYA
1963

Afro-Shirazi
revolution, 1964

EQUATORIAL GUINEA
1968

RWANDA
1960

BURUNDI
1960

ZANZIBAR
1963

Guerilla warfare against
Portuguese 1964-74

TANGANYIKA 1961
(United Republic of
TANZANIA with
ZANZIBAR, 1964)

Plebiscite, 1961, in British
Cameroons: north joins
Nigeria; south joins
Cameroun.

KATANGA
(Secedes from
Congo 1960-1963)

socialist-led rebellion,
1956-60

COMOROS
1975

Guerilla warfare against Portuguese,
1961-74; civil war in 1975 between
rival liberation movements (MPLA,
FNLA & UNITA).

ANGOLA
1975

MALAWI
1964

MOZAMBIQUE 1975

ZAMBIA
1964

ZIMBABWE
1980

MALAGASY
REPUBLIC
1960

SOUTH-WEST
AFRICA
(NAMIBIA)

BOTSWANA
1966

SWAZILAND
1968

SOUTH AFRICA

LESOTHO
1966

guerilla warfare
1966-1980

1947 rebellion
against the French

0   400   800   1600   1800   km

At independence African states had high hopes for the future. Freed from the shackles of colonial rule, they believed that they would achieve rapid economic growth, and that together they would exercise a decisive and constructive influence in world affairs. The reality of independence proved a severe disappointment in a number of ways:

a) Economic progress was held back because African countries continued to trade with the rich countries of the world on the same unequal terms as they had done during the colonial period – i.e. selling raw materials in exchange for industrial manufactures. Foreign aid was either too small, or else was used on schemes which helped the donor rather than the African recipients.

b) Africa was unable to act as a neutral or 'non-aligned' bloc, distinct from the Communist and Western worlds alike. Many African countries closely identified themselves with one side or the other, with the result that at the United Nations (set up in 1945) Africans could not speak with one voice. Nor could they agree on how best to deal with the surviving white-ruled states of South Africa and Rhodesia (now Zimbabwe).

c) Cooperation between African states was further harmed by border disputes between neighbours, caused by the often irrational frontiers inherited from the colonial period. Most serious has proved the conflict in the Horn of Africa between Ethiopia and Somalia. The OAU (Organisation of African Unity, founded in 1963) had great difficulty in acting as an effective mediator in such disputes.

d) African states were also weakened by civil wars, i.e. attempts to take over the government or to secede and form an independent state. Major wars occurred in Ethiopia (since 1961), Sudan (1963–72), Chad (since 1965) and Nigeria (1967–70). Only in the case of Sudan was mediation by the OAU successful.

e) Most states experienced military coups. In many cases this made little difference to the way the country was run; but in some cases major changes followed. In Libya (1969) and Ethiopia (1974) the soldiers ended the monarchy and proclaimed a socialist revolution. In Uganda (1971) Amin began a reign of terror which gravely damaged the country's economic and educational life. He was eventually removed by a Tanzanian military invasion (1979).

But although the ambitious hopes of the early 1960s were not fulfilled, independence did bring important changes. Education expanded enormously (including the creation of many new universities). Transport (especially roads)

attracted a great deal of investment. A few countries – notably Kenya and Ivory Coast – achieved a modest prosperity based on agriculture and light industry. Tanzania adopted in 1965 (the Arusha Declaration) an African form of socialism which has attracted world-wide attention. The African continent continues to show the same diversity which has characterised all her recent history.

Key to map

▪ Areas of most rapid economic development
• Major cities

The following are some of the more important military coups:
Algeria 1965
Benin 1972
Burundi 1976
Central African Republic 1979
Chad 1975
Comoros 1978
Congo 1968, 1977
Egypt 1952
Equatorial Guinea 1979
Ethiopia 1974
Ghana 1966, 1972, 1979
Guinea – Bissau 1980
Liberia 1979
Libya 1969
Malagasy 1975
Mauritania 1978
Nigeria 1966, 1975
Rwanda 1973
Somalia 1969
Sudan 1958, 1969
Uganda 1971
Upper Volta 1960, 1980
Zaire 1965

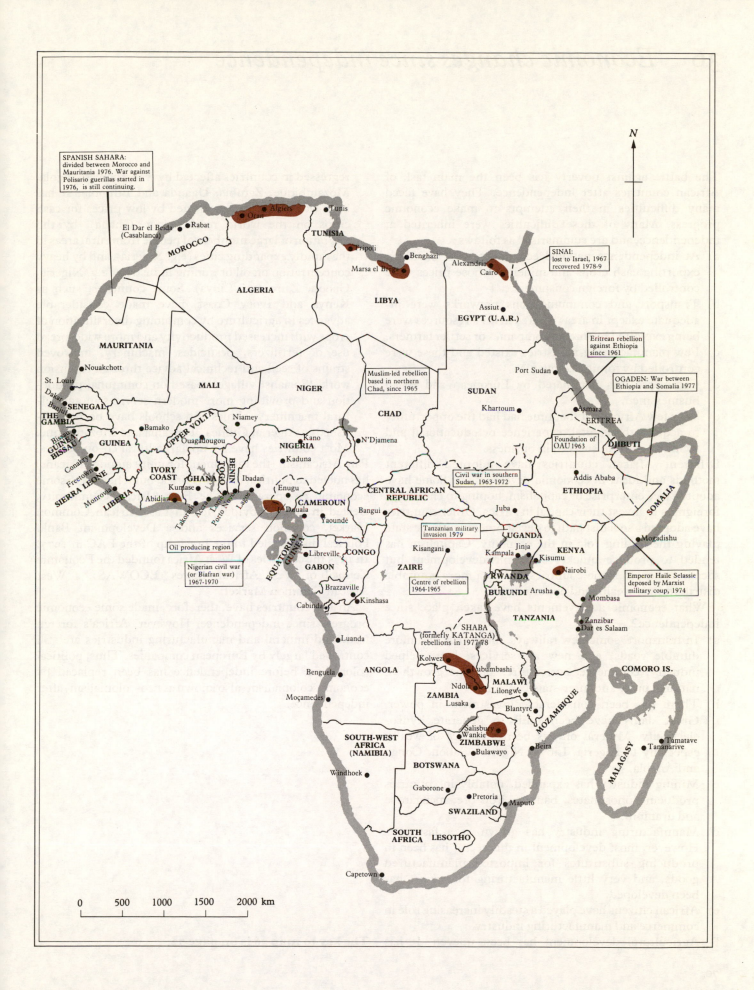

N

SPANISH SAHARA:
divided between Morocco and
Mauritania 1976. War against
Polisario guerillas started in
1976, is still continuing.

El Dar el Beida
(Casablanca)
Rabat

Algiers
Oran

Tunis

MOROCCO

TUNISIA

Tripoli

Marsa el Brega
Benghazi

Alexandria
Cairo

SINAI:
lost to Israel, 1967
recovered 1978-9

ALGERIA

LIBYA

MAURITANIA

Nouakchott

Assiut

EGYPT (U.A.R.)

Eritrean rebellion
against Ethiopia
since 1961

St. Louis

Dakar
Banjul
SENEGAL

THE
GAMBIA

Bissau
GUINEA-
BISSAU

Conakry

Freetown
SIERRA LEONE

Monrovia
LIBERIA

MALI

Bamako

NIGER

CHAD

Niamey

UPPER VOLTA

Ouagadougou

GUINEA

IVORY
COAST

GHANA

Kumase

Abidjan

Takoradi
Accra

TOGO
BENIN

Kano
NIGERIA

Kaduna

Ibadan

Lagos
Porto Novo

Enugu

Duala

N'Djamena

Muslim-led rebellion
based in northern
Chad, since 1965

SUDAN

Port Sudan

Khartoum

Asmara

ERITREA

Addis Ababa

ETHIOPIA

OGADEN: War between
Ethiopia and Somalia 1977

Foundation of
OAU 1963

DJIBOUTI

CAMEROUN

Yaoundé

CENTRAL AFRICAN
REPUBLIC

Bangui

Civil war in southern
Sudan, 1963-1972

Juba

Oil producing region

Nigerian civil war
(or Biafran war)
1967-1970

EQUATORIAL
GUINEA

Libreville

GABON

Brazzaville

Kinshasa

Cabinda

CONGO

ZAIRE

Kisangani

Centre of rebellion
1964-1965

Tanzanian military
invasion 1979

UGANDA

Kampala
Jinja
Kisumu

RWANDA

BURUNDI

Arusha

KENYA

Nairobi

Mombasa

Mogadishu

SOMALIA

Emperor Haile Selassie
deposed by Marxist
military coup, 1974

Luanda

SHABA
(formerly KATANGA)
rebellions in 1977-78

Kolwezi

Lubumbashi

Ndola

ZAMBIA

Lusaka

TANZANIA

Zanzibar
Dar es Salaam

COMORO IS.

Benguela

ANGOLA

Moçamedes

MALAWI
Lilongwe

Blantyre

MOZAMBIQUE

Salisbury
Wankie
ZIMBABWE

Bulawayo

Beira

MALAGASY

Tamatave
Tananarive

SOUTH-WEST
AFRICA
(NAMIBIA)

Windhoek

BOTSWANA

Gaborone

Pretoria

Maputo

SWAZILAND

SOUTH
AFRICA

LESOTHO

Capetown

0   500   1000   1500   2000 km

36 *Economic changes since independence*

The battle against poverty has been the main task of African countries after independence. They have faced many difficulties in their attempts to make economic progress. Many of these difficulties were inherited at independence, and are summarised as follows:

a) At independence national economies were based on exporting cash crops and minerals whose prices were controlled by foreign consumers.

b) Transport and communications networks were inadequate except in areas where Africa's resources were being exploited by foreign companies or settler farmers.

c) Few manufacturing industries existed and these were controlled by foreign companies.

d) Commerce was dominated by European and Asian businessmen.

e) Very few Africans at that time had had the opportunity to acquire the capital, experience or educational and technical skills to succeed in business.

Different African countries have adopted different methods and ideas in economic development. Some have adopted free enterprise or capitalism, hoping to encourage foreigners to invest their capital in Africa. Other countries have adopted a socialist path to development, with the state playing the leading role in the economy. Capitalism has tended to produce quicker economic development but socialism has, in some countries, led to a more equitable distribution of wealth and opportunities.

What economic achievements have taken place since independence?

a) In transport, some new railways, many new and more durable roads, and new air services, have helped industry, commerce, agriculture, and the growth of national unity and inter-state contacts.

b) There has been considerable investment in power. Great dams have been built to generate hydroelectricity. Mineral oil has been a source of wealth especially to Algeria, Libya, Nigeria, Gabon, Congo and Angola.

c) Mining industry has expanded, notably in countries producing phosphates, bauxite, iron ore, manganese and uranium.

d) Manufacturing industry has grown at a fast rate. However, most development in this sector has been in producing substitutes for imported manufactured goods, and very little manufacturing for export has been developed.

e) African citizens have played a steadily increasing role in commerce and manufacturing industry.

f) Agricultural development has been uneven. It has regressed in countries affected by war, such as Angola, Mozambique, Zambia, Uganda and Ethiopia. It has been slow in countries affected by low prices for cash crops on the world market (e.g. Ghana), by the migration of large numbers of people from rural areas to the rapidly expanding cities (e.g. Nigeria), and by heavy concentration on oil or mining industries (e.g. Nigeria, Gabon, Zaire and Libya). Some countries, such as Kenya and Ivory Coast, have made considerable advances in agriculture by combining diversification of crops with increased productivity and more widespread use of fertilizers, pesticides, machinery, improved strains of seed and technical advice through extension work. 'Socialist villages' based on communal production and providing more modern services in agricultural machinery, clinics and schools have been established in Algeria, Guinea, Tanzania and Mozambique. Most countries have set up agricultural co-operatives.

Pan-Africanism (the movement for unity among Africans) has not led to political unity in Africa, but it has led to some economic co-operation. The East African Community, created in 1967, provided for an East African Common Market, common services and a Development Bank. Political disputes led to the break-up of the EAC in 1977. In 1975 the countries of West Africa founded the Economic Council of West African States (ECOWAS), a West African Common Market.

African countries have, therefore, made some economic progress since independence. However, Africa's foreign trade and mineral and manufacturing industries are still controlled largely by European companies. Thus, political colonialism before independence has been replaced by economic colonialism (also known as neo-colonialism) after independence.

The key to map 36 is on page 72.

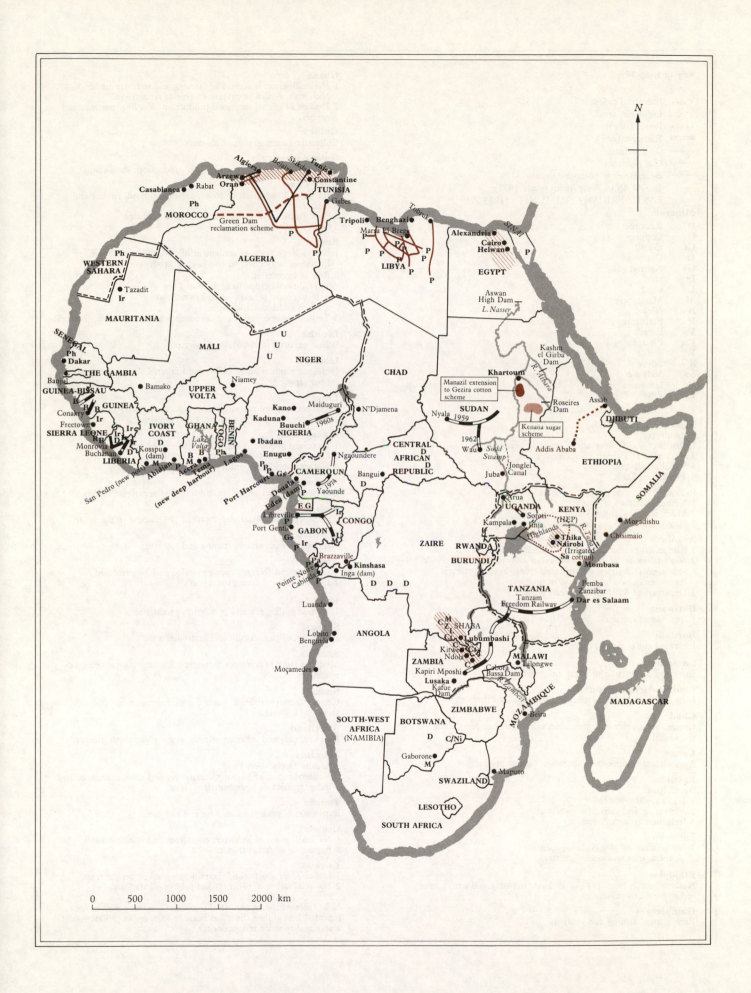

N

Algiers
Arzew Oran
Casablanca ● Rabat
MOROCCO
Ph
Bejaia Skikda Tunis
Constantine
TUNISIA
Gabes
Green Dam
reclamation scheme
P
Tripoli Benghazi
Marsa El Brega
P P P
P P
LIBYA
P
P
Tobruk

Alexandria
Cairo
Helwan
P
EGYPT

WESTERN
SAHARA
Ph

Tazadit
Ir

MAURITANIA

Aswan
High Dam
L. Nasser

SINAI

SENEGAL
Ph
Dakar
THE GAMBIA
Banjul
GUINEA-BISSAU
B
B
Conakry
B
GUINEA
Ir
SIERRA LEONE
Ir
Ir
Freetown
R
Monrovia
Ir
D
Buchanan
LIBERIA
M

ALGERIA

U
U
U

MALI

NIGER

CHAD

Kashm
el Girba
Dam
R. Atbara

Khartoum

Manazil extension
to Gezira cotton
scheme
SUDAN
Nyala 1959
1962
Wau

Roseires
Dam
Assab

Kenana sugar
scheme
Addis Ababa

DJIBOUTI

ETHIOPIA

Bamako

UPPER
VOLTA

Niamey

Kano
Kaduna
IVORY
COAST
D
GHANA
B
Kosspu
(dam)
Abidjan
Lake
Volta
B
BENIN
TOGO
B M
Accra
P
Ph
Tema
Lagos
Lomé

Maiduguri
1960s
Bauchi
NIGERIA
Ibadan
Enugu

N'Djamena

Ngaoundere

CENTRAL
AFRICAN
REPUBLIC
D

Sidd
Swamp

Juba

Jonglei
Canal

SOMALIA

San Pedro (new port)
(new deep harbour)

P P
Gs
CAMEROUN
Douala
Edea (dam)
P
Yaounde
E.G
Libreville
Port Gentil
Gs
GABON
P Ir
P
Brazzaville
P P
Pointe Noire
Cabinda
Kinshasa
Inga (dam)

Bangui

CONGO
Ir
1974
M

ZAIRE

RWANDA
BURUNDI

Arua
UGANDA
Soroti
Kampala
Jinja
Highlands

KENYA
(HEP)

Thika
Nairobi
(Irrigated
Sa cotton)

Mogadishu

Chisimaio

Mombasa

D D D

Luanda

Lobito
Benguela

ANGOLA

TANZANIA
Tanzam
Freedom Railway

Pemba
Zanzibar
Dar es Salaam

Moçamedes

M
C/Z SHABA
C/L
C Lubumbashi
Kitwe C
Ndola
ZAMBIA
Kapiri Mposhi
Lusaka
Kafue
Dam

Cabora
Bassa Dam
R. Zambezi

MALAWI
Lilongwe

SOUTH-WEST
AFRICA
(NAMIBIA)
D

BOTSWANA
C/Ni

ZIMBABWE

Beira

MOZAMBIQUE

MADAGASCAR

Gaborone
M

SWAZILAND
Maputo

LESOTHO
SOUTH AFRICA

0   500   1000   1500   2000 km

Key to map 36

Minerals

B	Bauxite
C	Copper
Ct	Cobalt
D	Diamonds
Gs	Natural gas
Ir	Iron
L	Lead
M	Manganese
N	Nickel
P	Petroleum
Pa	Potash
Ph	Phosphates
R	Rutile
S	Silver
Sa	Soda ash
U	Uranium
Z	Zinc

Algeria
Agriculture:
1 Distribution of white settler lands to peasants.
2 Marketing and credit co-operatives.
3 Socialist villages.
4 The Green Dam.

Industry:
1 Nationalisation.
2 Much workers' control.
3 Heavy industry: gas, petroleum and textiles.

Angola
1 Rise in oil production in the Cabinda enclave.
2 Nationalisation of coffee production and marketing of textile and sugar industries, and of retail trade. Foreign control continues in oil and diamond mining.
3 Departure of 350,000 European settlers.

Botswana
Expansion of cattle ranching and beef exports.

Burundi
Increased coffee production.

Cameroun
Increased production of sugar and bananas.

Central African Republic
Increased production of alluvial diamonds and timber.

Chad
Cotton, sugar, rice and groundnuts development programmes in the south.

Congo
Agricultural co-operatives increased timber production.

Egypt
Agriculture:
1 Land re-distribution.
2 Marketing and credit co-operatives.
3 Irrigation area extended.

Industry:
1 Nationalisation alongside capitalism.
2 Textiles, iron and steel, fertilisers.

Ethiopia
Nationalisation from 1974 of all land, industry and banks: land redistributed to peasants.

Gambia
Rice, cotton, fishing and tourism.

Ghana
1 Nationalisation of sectors of farming and industry under Nkrumah; return to private enterprise since 1966.
2 Decline of cocoa; increased production of coffee, bananas and rubber.

Guinea
Collective farms; export of alumina.

Guinea-Bissau
Increased potatoes, beans and soya production; state shops.

Ivory Coast
1 Increased production of cocoa, coffee, palm oil, rubber and timber.
2 New crops: pineapples, sugar, bananas and rice.
3 Growth of tourism.

Kenya
1 Kenya Highlands: re-settlement of 500,000 landless on European settler farms; rise in crop production.
2 Rise in exports of:
   a Traditional crops like coffee and tea.
   b New crops: pineapples and pyrethrum.
   c Meat and hides and skins.
3 Tourism: game parks, coastal beaches and mountains.

Lesotho
Wheat exports, road building, tourism.

Liberia
Increased production of coffee and timber; Liberianisation of rubber farming.

Libya
Social services: oil revenues have been used partly in massive expenditure on health, education and housing.

Madagascar
1 Increased production of coffee, cloves and vanilla.
2 Land reform: nationalisation of large farms.
3 Nationalisation of banking and import/export trade.

Malawi
Increased production on tea, tobacco and sugar plantations.

Mali
Cotton, rice and maize development programme in the south.

Morocco
Expansion of phosphate mining and tourism.

Nigeria
1 Industry and foreign trade expanded and Nigerianised.
2 Decline in food crop production.

Rwanda
Increased coffee, tea and pyrethrum production.

Senegal
Expansion of rice, cotton and groundnuts.

Somalia
Modernisation of livestock farming; meat canning factories; co-operatives.

Sudan
Cotton, forestry, fishing. Some denationalisation but public sector still dominant.

Swaziland
Iron ore, coal and asbestos mining; sugar plantations, timber.

Tanzania
1 Arusha Declaration 1967.
2 Nationalisation of banking, insurance, and most commerce and industry; ujamaa (communal) villages.

Tunisia
Expansion of phosphate mining and tourism.

Uganda
1 Nationalisation of industry, commerce and banking 1969.
2 Expulsion of Asian traders 1972.

Zaire
1 Increased production of the minerals marked on the map.
2 Nationalisation of palm oil and rubber plantations.

N.B. Information shown on the colonial economy map is not repeated here unless there has been an increase in production of a commodity since independence.

Index

References throughout are to page numbers.
Geographical features, towns etc. are printed like this : Adale
Countries, provinces and states are printed like this : ARABIA
Individual people are printed like this : *Stanley, H. M.*
Peoples, religions and languages are printed like this : *CREOLES*
The following abbreviations are used :

C. Cape   I., Is. Islands   L. Lake   Mt. Mount   R. River   S. Saint, Sao

Aba, 29, 61
Abadla, 59
Abd al Kader, 47
Abdullahi, Khalifa, 28
Abeokuta, 33, 35
Abidjan, 55, 61
ABOH, 14
Abomey, 33
Aborigines Rights Protection Society, 55
Aburi, 35
ACHOLI, 19
Accra, 13, 33, 35, 49, 55, 61
ADAL, 9
Adale, 47
ADAMAWA, 33
Adamawa Highlands, 1
Addis Ababa, 29, 47, 59, 69
Aden, 5, 27, 59
Aden, Gulf of, 1
ADRAR DES IFORAS, 47
Adwa, 4, 6, 47
African Association, 34
African National Congress, 64
Afrikaner (Boer) Nationalist Party, 64
AFRO-ASIATIC (ERYTHRAIC) languages, 2, 3
Afro-Shirazi revolution, 67
Agades, 11, 15, 35, 49
Agadir, 7, 47
Agaja, King, 16
AGAU, 4
Agordat, 59
Agouz, 7
Agulhas C., 1
Ahaggar, Mt., 1
Ahmad, Mohammed, 28
Aidhab, 5
AIR, 1, 11
Ajedabi, 47
AKAN, 3, 14
Akassa, 35
Akropong, 35
AKWAMU, 14, 15
AKYEM, 14, 15, 33
Al Baida, 29
ALAWITES, 6
ALBANY, 43
Albert L., 1
Albertville, 63
Alexandria, 5, 21, 47, 59
Algeria, 6, 46, 47, 49, 57, 58, 59, 66, 67, 72
Algiers, 4, 7, 47, 59
Ali, Mohammed, 28, 46
Ali al-Sanusi, Muhammed bin, 28
ALLADA (ARDRAH), 14, 15
ALMOHADS, 4, 5
ALMORAVIDS, 4, 5
ALULA, 47
ALUR, 19
ALWA, 4, 5, 8
Amba Alagi, 47
Amboina, 23
Ambrizete, 39
American Colonisation Society, 30
AMHARA, 3, 5, 29

Anglo-Boer War, 44
ANGLO-EGYPTIAN SUDAN, 57
Angoche, 20, 24, 27
ANGOLA, 17, 22, 23, 30, 50, 51, 52, 53, 57, 67, 72
Angra Pequena, 51
Ankober, 29
ANYI, 14, 15
apartheid (separation), 64
ARABIA, 21, 27
ARABS, 3, 5, 20, 24, 27, 38, 46
Arguin Is., 7, 13
ARO, 14
Arochuka, 33, 55
Arusha, 63
Arusha Declaration, 68
Arzila, 7
Asaba, 35
ASANTE, 14, 15, 32, 33, 49, 55
Asmara, 47, 59
Assab, 47
Assinie, 13
Assiut, 69
Aswan, 4, 5, 9, 29, 59
Aswan Dam, 59
Asyut, 59
Atbara, 47, 59
Atbara R., 47
Atebubu, 33
Atlas Mts., 4, 47
Audaghosi, 11
Aujila, 7, 11
AUSSA, 9
Awlil, 11
Axim, 13, 33
AXUM, Axum, 4, 5, 59
Azagal, 4
AZANDE, 3, 53
AZGER, 29
Azores Is., 13

BABUA, 53
Badagri, 13, 33, 35
Badi Abu Shillukh, 8
Bagamoyo, 39, 41
BAGIRMI, 14, 15, 29, 33
BAHR AL GHAZAL, 29
Baikia, Dr. William, 34, 35
BAILUNDO, 53
Baker, Sir Samuel, 40
Balearic Is., 1
Bamako, 33, 35, 49, 55, 61
BAMBARA STATES, 14
Banadir Coast, 20
BANDA, 3
Banda Is., 21, 23
Bangassou, 63
Bangui, 63
Bangweulu L., 1
BANTU, 2, 3, 18, 20, 26
BANTUSTANS, 64, 65
BAOL, 14, 15, 33
BAOULE, 55
Barbarossa, 6
BARBARY CORSAIRS, 6
Bardera, 47
Baro, 61

BAROTSE, 53
BAROTSELAND, 51, 52
Barth, Heinrich, 34, 35
BASHI, 53
BASOTHO, 53
Basra, 21
BASSA, 53
BASUTOLAND, 42, 43, 44, 45, 51, 57, 65
Batavia, 23
Bathurst, 30, 31, 33, 35, 49
BAULE, 14, 15
BECHUANALAND, 44, 45, 51, 53, 57, 65
Beira, 63
BEJA, 3
BELGIAN CONGO, 57, 61, 65
BEMBA, 3, 19, 39
BENADIR, 29, 47
Benghazi, 47, 59
Benguela, 23, 39, 41, 51, 63
BENIN, Benin, 10, 11, 15, 33, 49, 55, 61, 67
Benin, Bight of, 13
Benue R., 1
Berbera, 5, 21, 24, 27, 29, 47
BERBERISTAN (NUBIA), 9
BERBERS, 3, 4, 5, 6, 29, 46
Berlin Conference (1884–5), 48
Bethanie, 41
Bethune, 41
Bey, Ali, 9
Biafran War, 69
BIDA, 55
Bihé, 39, 41
Bilma, 11
BISA, 19, 38, 39
Bisandugu, 33, 49
Bismark, Count von, 48, 50
Bissao, 33, 49
Bissau, 13
Bizerta, 47, 59
Black Volta R., 1
Blantyre, 41, 63
Blood R., 42, 43
Blue Nile, R., 1
BOBANGI, 39
Bobo-Dioulasso, 33, 61
Bocarro, Gaspar, 27
Boer War, Anglo-, 44
Boer War, Xhosa-, 25, 26
BOERS, 26, 42, 43, 44
Bolobo, 39
Bombay, 23
BONDU, 14, 15, 33
Bonduku, 15, 33
Bone, 7, 47, 59
BONNY, Bonny, 14, 15, 33, 35
BONO, 10, 11, 15
Bonsu, Osei, 32
Boomplaats, 43
BORGU, 10, 11, 15, 33, 55
BORKU, 29
BORNEO, 21, 23
BORNO, 49, 55
Botha, 64
BOTSWANA, 67, 72

Bouake, 61
Bougie, 4, 7
BOURBON (later REUNION), 23, 24, 27
BRASS, Brass, 14, 15, 33, 35, 55
Brava, 9, 20, 47
BRAZIL, 17, 30, 31
Brazzaville, 51, 63
BRITISH BECHUANALAND, 44, 45
BRITISH CAMEROONS, 57, 67
BRITISH CENTRAL AFRICA, 51, 52, 53
BRITISH EAST AFRICA, 51, 52, 53
British East Africa Company, 51, 63
BRITISH KAFFRARIA, 43
BRITISH SOMALILAND, 47, 57, 59
British South Africa Company, 50, 52, 63
BRITISH WEST AFRICA, 54, 55
Broken Hill, 63
Bubakir, 35
Buchanan, 61
BUDJA, 53
BUGANDA, 18, 39, 40, 41, 51, 52, 53
Bulawayo, 37, 51, 63
Bunkeya, 41
BUNYORO, 18, 19, 39, 51, 53
BURMA, 21
BURMI, 55
Burton, Sir Richard, 40
BURUNDI, 18, 19, 39, 51, 67, 72
BUSHMANOIDS, 2
BUSSA, Bussa, 10, 33, 35, 47, 49, 55

CABINDA, 51, 57
Caillie, Rene, 34
Cairo, 4, 5, 9, 21, 29, 59
CALABAR, 14, 15, 33, 35
Calcutta, 23
Caledon R., 43
Calicut, 23
CAMEROUN, 57, 62, 67, 72
Canary Is., 1, 13, 59
Cape Blanco, 13
Cape Bojado, 13
Cape Coast, 13, 33, 35, 49
CAPE COLONY, 26, 41, 42, 43, 44, 45, 51
CAPE PROVINCE, 65
Cape Town, 23, 25, 63, 65
Cape Verde Is., 1, 13, 23
Caprivi Strip, 51
Casablanca, 47, 59
cash-crop farming, 32, 33, 58, 59, 60, 61, 62, 63
Catholic Missionary Societies, 34, 40, 41
cattle trade, 32, 33
CAUCASOIDS, 2
CAYOR, 14, 15, 33, 55
Central African Federation, 66
CENTRAL AFRICAN REPUBLIC, 67, 72
Ceuta Tetuan, 4, 7, 47, 59
CEWA, 53

CEYLON, 21, 23
CHAD, 49, 51, 67, 68, 69, 72
Chad L., 1
CHAGGA SHAMBAA, 39
CHANGAMIRE, 18, 19, 37
Charleston, 31
Chilembwe, Rev. John, 52, 53
CHINA, 21
CHRISTIANS, 4, 5, 6, 7, 34, 35, 52
Christiansborg, 13
CHWEZI, 16
Clapperton, 34, 35
COKWE, 3, 38, 39
Colomb Bechar, 47, 59
Comoro Is., 1
COMOROS, 67
Conakry, 49, 61
'concession' system, 62, 63
CONGO, 67, 72
CONGO FREE STATE (later
    BELGIAN CONGO), 47, 50, 51,
    52, 53, 63, 66
Constantine, 7, 47
Cotonou, 49, 55, 61
CREOLES, 55
Crowther, Samuel Ajayi, 34
CUBA, 17, 31
CURACAO, 31
Cyrenaica, 7, 29, 47

Da Gama, Vasco, 13, 22, 23
DAGOMBA, 15, 33
Dahlak I., 5
DAHOMEY (later BENIN), 14, 15,
    32, 33, 49, 54, 55, 60, 61
Dakar, 31, 33, 35, 49, 61
Damascus, 5
Damietta, 5
DAMOT, 5
Danakil Coast, 47
Danakil Desert, 1
Dar es Salaam, 39, 51, 63
DARFUR, 9, 11, 29, 47
Darna, 47
De Brazza, 40, 48, 50
Delgado C., 20
DEMBOS, 53
Denham, Dixon, 34, 35
DENKYIRA, 14, 15
Diagne, Blaise, 55
diamonds, 44, 45, 60, 61, 64, 65
Dias, Bartholomeu, 13, 23
Diego Suarez, 63
Dilolo, 41
DINKA, 3
Diu, 23
Dixcove, 13
DJADO, 11
Djelfa, 59
Djerba I., 4, 7
Djibuti, 58, 59, 67
Djidjelli, 7
Dogali, 47
DONGOLA, Dongola, 5, 9, 29, 47
Douala, 41, 51, 63
Dragut, 6
Drakensberg Mts., 1, 37
Du, 5
Dulti, 35
Durban, 45, 63, 65
DYULA, 32

East African Community (EAC), 70
East London, 45, 63, 65
Ebrohimi, 33, 55
Economic Council of West African
    States (ECOWAS), 70, 71
Edward L., 1
EGBA, 32, 33, 55
Egga, 35
EGYPT, 5, 7, 8, 21, 28, 29, 47, 50, 56,
    57, 59, 67, 72
El Aaiun, 59
El Dar el Beida, 69
El Fasher, 29, 47

El Kasar, 7
El Kharga, 59
El Obeid, 29, 47, 58, 59
ELDAMER, 29
Elizabethville, 63, 65
Elmina, 13, 23, 35
EMBU, 39
ENNEDI, 29
Entebbe, 51, 63
Enugu, 61, 69
EQUATORIA, 29, 50
EQUATORIAL GUINEA, 67
ERITREA, 47, 56, 57, 59, 67, 69
ETHIOPIA, 8, 21, 23, 28, 46, 47, 56,
    57, 58, 59, 66, 67, 69, 72
Ethiopian Highlands, 1
Etinam, 35
EWE, 15
exports, 16, 17, 30, 32, 58, 59, 60

FANG, 3, 39, 53
FANTE, 14, 15, 32, 33, 54, 55
Faras, 5
Fashoda, 29, 47, 51
FATIMIDS, 4, 5
Fernando Po, 1, 13, 23, 51, 57, 67
Fez, 4, 7, 11, 47
FEZZA, 47
FEZZAN, 29
Figuig, 47
Firka, 47
Fodio, Uthman dan, 32
Fort Dauphin, 23
Fort Gouraud, 59
Fort James, 13
Fort Jameson, 37
Fort Lamy, 49
Francistown, 65
Freetown, 30, 31, 32, 33, 34, 41, 49, 55,
    61
FRENCH EQUATORIAL AFRICA,
    52, 53, 57, 61, 63
FRENCH GUINEA, 49, 54, 55, 61
FRENCH SOMALILAND, 47, 57, 59
FRENCH SUDAN, 49, 54, 55, 61
FRENCH WEST AFRICA, 47, 57
Freretown, 41
FULANI, 3, 14, 32
FUNJI, 8, 9, 29
FUR, 3, 8
FUTA JALON, 1, 14, 15, 32, 33, 49
FUTA TORO, 14, 15, 16, 33

Gaberones, 45
Gabes, 59
GABON, 30, 50, 51, 67
Gaborone, 63, 65
Gafsa, 7
GALLA, 3
Gallabat, 28, 29
GAMBIA, 30, 32, 33, 49, 55, 57, 61,
    67, 72
Gambia R., 1
GANDA, 3
Gao, 11, 15, 35, 49
Gaya, 33
GAZA, 37
Gedi, 20
Gedaref, 47
GERMAN EAST AFRICA, 48, 51,
    52, 53
German East Africa Company, 63
GERMAN SOUTH-WEST
    AFRICA, 48
Gezira cotton scheme, 59
Ghadames, 7, 11, 47
GHANA, 10, 67, 72
Ghat, 7, 11, 47
GIRIAMA, 53
Goa, 23
GOJJAM, 29
gold, 7, 20, 21, 44, 45, 60, 61, 64, 65
GOLD COAST, 12, 13, 32, 33, 49, 54,
    55, 57, 60, 61
Goldie, George, 48

Gondar, 9
Gondokoro, 29, 41
GONJA, 14, 15, 33
Good Hope C., 1
Goree I., 13
GOSHEN, 45
GRAAFF REINET, 25, 26
Grahamstown, 43, 45, 65
GRAIN COAST, 12, 13 ; *see also*
    LIBERIA
Gran, Ahmed, 8
GRANADA, Granada, 4, 7
Grand Bassam, 33, 49
Grand Ladu, 13
Grand Popo, 13, 35
Grant, James, 40
Great Fish R., 43
Great Trek, 42
GREBO, 15
Greenville, 35
GRIQUA, 25, 43
GRIQUALAND WEST, 44, 45
Grootfontein, 63
groundnuts, 31
GUINEA, 10, 49, 67, 72
GUINEA-BASSAU, 67, 72
'Gun War', 53
GUSH, 53
Gwandu, 33
GWANGARA NGONI, 37
Gwato, 13

HABASH, 9
HADRAMAUT, 21
HAFSIDS, 4
Haile Selassie, Emperor, 69
HAITI, 16
Hamdullani, 33
Hara, 29, 59
Harris, William Wade, 55
Hassan, Mohammed Abdilla, 46
HAUSA, 3, 10, 11, 14, 15, 32, 33
Hausaland, 60
HEHE, 37, 53
Henry, Prince, The Navigator, 12
HERERO, 3, 53
Hertzog, 64
High Atlas, 1
HIJAZ, 5
HLUBI, 36, 37
HOGGA, 11
Homs, 47
Horn of Africa desert, 1
horse trade, 32, 33
Hottentots, *see KHOIKHOI*
HUSSAINIDS, 6

Ibadan, 32, 33, 35, 61
Ibo I., 27
Ibrim, 5
Idah, 33
IFAT, 4
IFE, 10, 11, 15
IFNI, 47, 59
IGALA, 14, 15, 33
Igbebe, 35
IGBO, 3, 14, 15, 16, 33
Ijaye, 35
Ijebu, 49, 55
ILORIN, Ilorin, 32, 49, 55
IMBANGALA, 18, 19, 38, 39
IMERINA, 24, 27, 40, 41
In Salah, 47
INDIA, 21
Indian Ocean trade, 21
industrialisation, 64
Ingombe Ilede, 19
Inhambane, 23, 24, 27
International African Association, 50
Inyati, 41
Irebu, 41
Irebu, 39
iron, 20
Isandhlwana, 44, 45
ISEYIN, 55
ISLAM, 10, 20, 28

Ismail, Mulay, 6, 28, 46
Ismailia, 47, 59
ITALIAN SOMALILAND, 47, 57,
    59
ITALY, 21
ITSEKIRI, 33
ivory, 20, 21, 38
IVORY COAST, 12, 13, 49, 54, 55, 60,
    61, 67, 72

JAGA, 18, 19
Jaghbub, 29, 47
Jaja, King, 54
JAMAICA, 17, 31
Jameson raid, 44
JAPAN, 21
JAVA, 21, 23
Jebba, 61
Jebel Marga, 1
Jebel Qadir, 29
Jenne, 11, 32, 33
Jidda, 5
JIMMA, Jimma, 29, 59
Joal, 13
Johannesburg, 45, 51, 63, 65
John II, 22
Johnson, James, 34
JOLOF, 15, 33, 55
Jos, 61
Jos Plateau, 1
Juba, 47
Juba R., 1
JUBALAND, 47
JUKUN, 14, 15, 33

KAARTA, 15, 33
Kabarega Falls, 41
Kabylia, 47
Kader, Abd-el, 46
Kaduna, 61
KAFFA, 29
Kaffir, *see XHOSA*
Kafue R., 1
Kageyi, 39
Kairouan, 4, 7
Kalahari Desert, 1
KAMBA, 38, 39
KAMERUN, 48, 49, 51, 52, 53
Kampala, 63
KANEM, 29
KANEM-BORNO, 10, 11, 14, 15, 32,
    33
Kanemi, al-, 32
Kangaba, 11
Kankan, 33, 61
Kano, 11, 15, 32, 33, 35, 49, 55, 61
KANURI, 3
KARAGWE, 39
Kareima, 59
Kariba Dam, 63
KARONGA, Karonga, 39, 53
Kasai R., 1
KASANJE, Kasanje, 18, 19, 39, 41
Kasese, 63
Kasongo, 39, 41
Kassala, 47, 59
KATANGA (later SHABA), 41, 51,
    67, 69
Katsina, 33, 35
Kayes, 35, 49, 61
KAZEMBE, Kazembe, 18, 19, 39
Keetmansdorp, 63, 65
KENYA, 50, 57, 66, 67, 72
Keren, 47
Kerimba I., 20
Keta, 35
Khartoum, 28, 29, 41, 47, 58, 59
KHARTOUMERS, see SUDANESE
KHOIKHOI, 25, 26
KHOISAN language, 2, 3
Khufra, 29, 47
Kibanga, 41
Kigoma, 63
KIKUYU, 3, 39, 53
Kilifi, 20

Kilimanjaro Mt., 1
KILWA, Kilwa, 19, 20, 21, 23, 24, 39
Kilwa Kirinje, 27
Kilwa Kisiwani, 20
Kimberley, 45, 51, 63, 65
KIMBU, 37
Kindu, 63
King William's Town, 43
Kisangani, 69
Kisimayu, 20, 47, 59
KISSI, 55
Kisumu, 63
KITARA, 18
Kitw, 65
Kivu L., 1
Kizimkazi, 20
kola nuts, 32, 33
Kolobeng, 41
KOLOLO, 36, 37
Kommenda, 13
KONG, 15, 32, 33
KONGO, 3, 18, 19, 22, 23, 53
KORANA, 25
KORDOFAN, 9, 29
Kosti, 59
KOTA, 53
Kotakota, 39
Koulikoro, 35, 61
KPE, 53
Kroonstad, 65
KRU, 15
KUBA, 19
Kuka, 33, 35
KUMALO, 37
KUMASI, Kumasi, 32, 33, 49, 61
Kumbi Saleh, 11
Kunene R., 1
Kuruman, 41
Kwango R., 1
Kwanza R., 1
KWENA, 43
Kyoga L., 1

LABILELA, Labilela, 4, 5
LADO, 47, 51
Ladysmith, 43, 45, 65
Laghouat, 47
Lagos, 13, 32, 33, 35, 49, 55, 61
Laing, Maj., 34
LAMBA, 39
Landana, 29
Lander, Richard & John, 34, 35
languages, traditional, 2
Larache, 7
Las Navas de Tolosa, 4
LASTA, 5
League for the Rights of Man, 55
League of Nations, 56
Lealui, 19, 37, 39, 41
Leopold II, King, 48, 50
Leopoldsville, 51, 63
Lepanto, 7
LESOTHO (later BASUTOLAND), 36, 37, 43, 67, 72
LIBERIA, 30, 31, 32, 33, 49, 55, 57, 60, 61, 66, 72
Libreville, 30, 31, 41, 51
LIBYA, 56, 57, 58, 59, 67, 68, 72
Likoma, 41
Limpopo R., 1
Lisale, 39
Lisbon, 4, 23
Little Popo, 13
Livingstone, David, 40
Livingstonia, 41, 63
LOANGO, Loango, 19, 39
Lobbo, Ahmad, 32
Lokoja, 35
Lomami R., 1
Lome, 49, 55, 61
Lourenco Marques, 44, 45, 51, 63
L'Ouverture, Toussaint, 16
LOZI, 3, 18, 19, 39, 41
Lualaba R., 1
Luanda, 19, 23, 39, 41, 51, 63

Luangwa R., 1
Luapula R., 1
LUBA, 3, 18, 19, 53
Luderitz Bay, 63, 65
Lugh, 47
Lukolela, 41
Luluaborg, 63
LULUA, 39
LUNDA, 3, 18, 19, 38, 39
LUO, 3, 18, 19
Lusaka, 63
LUVALE, 19, 39

Macao, 23
MACINA, 15, 32, 33
MADAGASCAR, 1, 21, 23, 24, 40, 50, 51, 52, 53, 57, 72
MADEIRA, 13
Madras, 23
Mafeking, 45, 51, 65
Mafia I., 1, 20, 27
Magdala, 29
MAGHRIB (North-west Africa), 4, 58
Mahdia, 4
MAHDIS, 28, 46
Mait, 5
MAJERTEYN, 29
Maji, 29
Maji-Maji rebellion, 52, 53
Majuba Hill, 44, 45
MAKOMBE, 53
Makurdi, 61
MAKURIA, 45
MALABAR, 21
Malacca, 21, 23
MALAGASY, 2, 3, 53
Malan, 64
Malange, 63
MALAWI, 19, 67, 72
Malawi L., 1
MALI, 10, 13, 67, 72
Malindi, 23, 27
MALINKE, 3
MAMLUKS, 4, 5, 8
Manakara, 63
Manda, 20
mandated territories, 56, 57
MANDE, 10, 11, 15, 33
MANDINKA, 14, 15, 32, 55
Mansur, Al-, 6
MANTHAIISI, 37
Maputo, 65
Maradi, 33
Marico, 37, 42, 43
MAROONS, 16
Marrakesh, 4, 7, 11, 47, 59
Marseilles, 31
Marzuq, 7
MASAI, Masai, 3, 41
Masasi, 41
Mascara, 47
Mascarene Is., 23
MASEKO NGONI, 37
Masena, 35
Maseru, 65
MASHONALAND, 51
Massawa, 5, 9, 29, 47, 59
MATABELELAND, 51
Matadi, 63
Matam, 13
MATAMBA, 19
MATIWANE, 37
Mau Mau rebellion, 66, 67
MAURETANIA, 47, 49
MAURITANIA, 59, 67
MAURITIUS, 23, 24, 27
Mayumba, 39
Mazagan, 7
Mazrui family, 27, 53
Mbabane, 65
MbanzaKongo, 19
MBUNDU, 3
Mecca, 5, 21
Medina, 5, 21
Mekalle, 47

Meknes, 7, 47, 59
Melilla, 7, 47, 59
MENDE, 3
Menelik II, 28, 58
MERINA, 3, 53
MERINIDS, 4, 5
Merka, 47
Merowe, 4, 5
Mers el Kebir, 7
Mfecane period, 36, 37, 42
MFENGU (FINGO) 36, 37, 43, 45
MIDDLE CONGO, 51
MIDDLE NIGER, 14
migrant labour, 60, 61, 64
minerals, 19, 58, 59, 60, 61, 62, 63, 64, 65
Mining, 60
Minna, 61
Misurata, 59
Mizda, 29
Mocambique Company, 63
Mocamedes, 63
Mogadishu, 20, 47, 59
Molucca Is., 21, 23
Mombasa, 20, 22, 23, 24, 27, 39, 41, 51, 63
Mongalla, 47
MONGOLOIDS, 2
Monrovia, 31, 33, 35, 49, 61
Moree, 13
MOROCCO, 4, 6, 11, 47, 57, 58, 59, 67, 72
Morocco, Sultan of, 44
Moshi, 63
Moshoeshoe, 36
Mossel Bay, 65
MOSSI, 3, 10, 11, 15, 33, 55
MOURIDES, 55
MOZAMBIQUE, 19, 22, 23, 24, 27, 39, 45, 50, 51, 52, 53, 57, 61, 63, 67
Mpande, 42, 43
MPANGAZITA, 37
MPEZENI, 37
Mpinda, 23
MPONDO, 25, 37, 43, 45
MSIRI, 39
MTHETHWA, 36, 37
Mtwara, 63
MUGHAL EMPIRE, 23
Muhlenberg, 35
Mumin, Abd al, 4
Mungbere, 63
Muridiyya movement, 54
Murzuq, 11, 47
Muscat, 21, 27
MUSLIMS, 4, 5, 22, 54
Mwanza, 63
Mwato Yamyo, 19, 39
Mwene Mutapa (Monomotapa), 18, 19, 23
Mweru L., 1
Mzilikazi, 36, 37

Nairobi, 51, 63
Nakuru, 63
NAMA, 25, 53
Namib Desert, 1
NAMIBIA, 67
NANDI, 53
Nanyuki, 63
Nasser L., 1
NATAL, 42, 43, 44, 45, 51, 65
nationalism movements, 66, 67
natural crops, see cash-crop farming
NDEBELE, 36, 37, 42, 52, 53
Ndola, 63, 65
NDONGO, 19
NDWANDWE, 36, 37
NEGROES, 2
NEW CALIBAR, 14, 33
New Dongola, 29
New Orleans, 31
NEW REPUBLIC, 44, 45
New York, 31
Newcastle, 65

newspapers, 55
NGALA, 39
Ngazargamu, 11, 15, 33
NGONI, 37, 53
NGUNI 26, 36, 44
Nguru, 61
NGWANE, 36, 37
NGWATO, 43, 53
Nigni, 11
NIGER, 49, 54, 55, 61, 67
Niger R., 34
NIGER COAST PROTECTORATE, 48
Niger Delta, 1, 34, 48
NIGERIA, 49, 54, 55, 57, 61, 67, 68, 72
NIKKI, Nikki, 10, 49
Nile R., 1, 46
Nile Delta, 1
NILOTES, 16, 29
NILOTIC language, 2, 3
Nioro, 49
NKORE, 18, 19, 39
NORTHERN RHODESIA, 57, 66
Nouakchott, 59
Nova Libre, 63
NOVA SCOTIA, 17
Nqeto, 37
NUBA, 3
NUBIA, 4, 8
NUER, 3
NUPE, 10, 11, 14, 15
NXABA, 37
NYAMWEZI, 3, 37, 38, 39, 53
NYANJI, 53
NYASALAND, 50, 52, 65, 66
Nyassa Company, 63

OBBIA, 47
OGADEN, 53, 69
Ogbomasso, 35
Ogowe R., 1
OLD CALABAR, 14
Old Oyo, 33
OMAN, 21, 24, 27
Omdurman, 28, 29, 47
Onitsha, 33, 35
OPOBO, Opobo, 33, 54, 55
Oran, 4, 7, 47, 59
Orange R., 1
ORANGE FREE STATE, 42, 43, 44, 45, 51, 65
ORANGE RIVER COLONY (later ORANGE FREE STATE), 44
Organisation of African Unity (OAU), 68, 69
Orleansville, 47
Ormuz, 21
OROMO, 8, 9, 29
OTTOMAN (TURKISH) EMPIRE, 6, 8, 9, 24, 27
Ouagadugu, 61
Ouargla, 7
Oudney, 34, 35
Ouidah, 13, 14, 33, 35
OVIMBUNDU, 19, 38, 39
Owen Falls Dam, 63
OYO, 10, 11, 14, 15, 32, 33

palm oil, 60
Pan-African movement, 64, 66, 70, 71
Paraku, 61
Park, Mungo, 34, 35
Pasha, Arabi, 46
Pate I., 27
PEDI, 43
Pemba I., 20, 27
Penon de Velez, 7
PERSIA, 21
Philippolis, 43
Philippeville, 47
Pietermaritzburg, 43, 45, 65
Pietersburg, 45, 65
Podor, 13
Points Noire, 63

pombeiros, 38, 39
Pondicherry, 23
Ponthierville, 63
Port Elizabeth, 63, 65
Port Etienne, 59
Port Francqui, 63
Port Harcourt, 61
Port Natal (Durban), 43
Port Nolloth, 65
Port Said, 47, 59
Port Sudan, 47, 58, 59
Port Novo, 13, 33, 49
Portudal, 13
PORTUGAL, 7
PORTUGUESE EAST AFRICA, 42
PORTUGUESE GUINEA, 49, 55, 57, 61
Potchefstroom, 43, 45
Potoieter, 43
Pretoria, 43, 45, 51, 63
Pretoria Convention, 44
Pretorius, 43
Principe, 1, 13, 51, 57, 67
Protestant Missionary Societies, 34, 40, 41

QWABE, 37
QUARAMANLI, 6
QUEEN ADELAIDE PROVINCE, 43
Quelimane, 2, 4, 41
Quru, 29

Rabai, 41
Rabat, 4, 59
railways, 58, 59, 60, 61, 62, 63
Rand, 45
Red Sea, 1
Rejaf, 29
Retief, Piet, 43
Rhodes, Cecil, 44, 50
RHODESIA, 51, 52, 53 ; *see also* NORTHERN RHODESIA ; SOUTHERN RHODESIA
Rif, 47
Rio de Janeiro, 31
RIO DE ORO, 47, 57
RIO MUNI, 51
Robben I., 65
Roberts, J. J., 30
Roseires, 59
Rovuma R., 1
Royal Niger Company, 48
ROZWI, 37
RUANDA-URUNDI, 57
Rubaga, 41
rubber, 60
Rukwa L., 1
RWANDA, 18, 19, 39, 51, 67, 72

SAADIANS, 6
Sabi R., 1
Safi, 7, 59
SAHARA, 10
Sahara Desert, 1
Said, Sayyid, 24, 27
S. Catherine Cape, 13
S. Louis, 13, 33, 35, 49, 61
S. Mary, 23
S. Salvador, 19, 23, 41
S. Tomé, 1, 13, 17, 23, 31, 51, 57, 67
SAKALAVA, 3, 27
Salaga, 33
Salisbury, 51, 63
Salisbury, Lord, 50
SAMORI, 33, 54, 55
SAN (BUSHMEN), 25, 26
Sanaga R., 1
Sand R., 43
Sanga, 19
SANGU, 37
SANHAJA, 4
Santo Domingo, 17
SANUSI, 28, 29, 46, 47
SARRAKOLE, 55

SAY, Say, 15, 29, 35, 49
SEBETWANE, 36, 37
SEGU, Segu, 14, 15, 33, 35, 49, 55
Sekondi-Takoradi, 61
Sena, 23, 24, 27
SENEGAL, 32, 33, 49, 54, 55, 60, 61, 67, 72
Senegal R., 1
SENEGAMBIA, 10
Senna, 5, 59
Sennar, 9, 29
Sesheke, 19
Setif, 4
Seville, 4
Sfax, 4, 47, 59
SHABA, 69
Shaka, 36
Shama, 13
SHANGANE, 53
Sharpeville, 65
Shaykan, 29
Shebelle R., 1
SHENDI, 9, 29
Shengeh, 35
SHIRAZI, 20
Shire R., 1
SHOA, 9, 29
SHONA, 3, 39, 52, 53
SICILY, 4, 7
SIDAMO, 29
SIERRA LEONE, 13, 30, 31, 32, 33, 34, 49, 54, 55, 57, 61, 67
Sijilmasa, 4, 7, 11
Sikasso, 33, 55
SINAI, 1, 69
Siraf, 21
Siwa, 47
SLAVE COAST, 12, 13, 14
slave trade, 16, 17, 24, 27, 30
Soba, 5
SOBHUZA, 37
Socotra, 23, 27
Sofala, 20, 21, 23, 24, 27
Sokoto, 33, 35, 49, 55
SOKOTO CALIPHATE, 32, 33, 55
SOLOMONIDS, 4
SOMALI, 3, 27, 46
SOMALIA, 56, 67, 68, 72
Songea, 37
SONGHAI, 10, 14, 15
SONGYE, 19
SOSHANGANE, 36, 37
SOTHO, 3, 25, 26, 36
SOUTH AFRICA, UNION OF, 52, 53, 56, 57, 64, 65, 67
South African Native National Congress, 53
SOUTH AFRICAN REPUBLIC (later TRANSVAAL), 43, 44, 45, 51
SOUTH-WEST AFRICA (later NAMIBIA), 44, 51, 52, 53, 57, 65, 67
SOUTHERN NIGERIA, 60
SOUTHERN RHODESIA, 44, 57, 66
SPAIN, 7
SPANISH GUINEA, 57
SPANISH MOROCCO, 47
SPANISH SAHARA, 47, 49, 59, 67, 69
Speke, J. H., 40
Stanley, H. M., 40, 48, 50
Stanley Falls, 1, 51
Stanley Pool, 41
Stanleyville, 63
STELLALAND, 45
Stellenbosch, 25
Stevenson Road, 41
Suakin, 5, 9, 29, 47
SUDAN, 10, 28, 46, 47, 56, 57, 67, 68, 69
SUDAN, ANGLO-EGYPTIAN, 51, 57, 59
SUDANESE, 6, 38
Sudd Swamp, 29, 59
Suez, 59

Suez Canal, 29, 47, 59
SUMATRA, 21, 23
Surat, 23
Sus, 47, 59
SWAHILI, 3, 38
Swahili coast, 22, 24, 50, 53
Swakopmund, 51
SWAZI, 37, 43
SWAZILAND, 44, 45, 51, 57, 65, 67, 72
Swellendam, 25, 26
SYRIA, 21

Tabora, 39, 41, 51, 63
Tadmekka, 11, 15
Tafilaler, 7
Tafna, Treaty of, 46
Taghaza, 7, 11
Takedda, 11, 15
Tamatave, 63
Tamenrasset, 47
Tana L., 1
Tana R., 1
Tananarive, 41, 51, 63
TANGANYIKA, 57, 62, 67
Tanganyika L., 1
Tangier, 7, 47, 59
TANZANIA, 67, 68, 72
Taoudeni, 7, 11
Taroudant, 4
Taza, 7
TEGALE, 9
TEKE, 19, 39
TEKRUR, 10, 11
Tel el kebir, 47
Tenes, 7
TEMBU, 25, 37, 43, 45, 53
TEMNE, 15
TEMNE-MENDE, 55
Tete, 23, 24, 27, 39
Tewadras, 28
Thaba Bosiu, 36, 37
Thies, 61
THLAPING, 43
Thomson, J., 40
TIBESTI, 11, 29
Tibesti Mts., 1
Tidsi, 7
TIGRE, 29
Timbuktu, 7, 11, 13, 15, 32, 33, 35, 49
Tindouf, 47
Tinmel, 4
Tippu Tib, 38, 39, 52, 53
Tlemcen, 4, 7, 47
Tobruq, 47
TOGO, 48, 49, 54, 55, 67
TOGOLAND, 57, 61
TOKOLOR, 14, 33, 55
Toledo, 4
TONGA, 19
TONGALAND, 44, 45
TORO, 39
Toure, Samori, 32
trade routes, 10, 17, 20, 21, 32, 33
TRANSKEI, 64, 65
TRANSVAAL, 42, 43, 44, 65
TREKBOERS, 25
Tripoli, 4, 6, 7, 11, 47, 59
TRIPOLITANIA, 29, 46, 47
TSONGA, 43
TSWANA, 3, 25
TUAREG, 3, 14, 15, 55
Tuat, 7, 11
Tugela R., 43
Tuggart, 7, 47, 59
Tumart, Ibn, 4
TUMBWE, 19
Tunis, 4, 7, 11, 46, 59
TUNISIA, 47, 57, 58, 59, 67, 72
TUNJUR, 9
Turkana L., 1
TURKISH EMPIRE, 6, 8
Tushki, 29
TUTA NGONI, 37

Ubangi R., 1
UBANGI-CHARI, 51
UGANDA, 50, 51, 52, 53, 57, 62, 67, 68, 72
Uganda Protectorate, 52
Ujiji, 41
Ulundi, 45
UMAR, 32
Umar, Al Hajj, 32
Umtata, 65
Unyanyembe, 39
Upoto, 41
UPPER NIGER, 14, 33
UPPER VOLTA, 55, 61, 67

Vaal R., 1
VENDA, 43
Vereoniging, 45, 65
Victoria, 41
Victoria Falls, 1, 19
Victoria L., 1
Viervoet, 43
Villa Cabral, 63
Villa Serpa Pinto, 63
Volta L., 1
von Wissman, 40
Vryheid, 45

Wad Medani, 47
WADAI, 11, 29
Wadan, 7, 11
Wadi Halfa, 29, 47, 59
Wadja, 47
Wagedugu, 33, 49
Walatu, 7, 11
Walvis Bay, 51, 63
WANGARA (BAMBUK), 10, 11
Wankie, 53, 63
Wargla, 47
Warri, 13
Warsheik, 47
Wawa, 35
White Nile R., 15, 41
white settlers, 62, 66
White Volta R., 1
Windhoek, 41, 63
Witu, 51
Witwatersrand, 44
WOLOF, 3, 10, 11, 14

XHOSA, 3, 25, 26, 37, 42, 43

YAKA, 53
YAO, 3, 38, 39, 53
Yaounde, 63
Yasin, Ibn, 4
YEKE, see NYAMWEZI
YEMEN, 5, 9, 21
Yendi, 33
Yohannis IV, 28
Yola, 33, 35
YORUBA, 32
YORUBALAND, 32, 33

Zagora, 7
ZAGWE, 4
ZAIRE, 67, 72
Zaire R., 1, 23, 50
Zambezi R., 1, 22
ZAMBIA, 67
ZANZIBAR, 50, 51, 53, 67
Zanzibar Is., 20, 23, 24, 27, 41
Zaria, 33, 35, 61
ZAYANIDS, 4
Zeila, 5, 9, 21, 24, 27, 29, 47
ZIMBA, 24, 27
ZIMBABWE, Zimbabwe, 19, 66, 67
Zindar, 35, 49, 61
Zoutpansberg, 43
ZULUS, 3, 42, 43, 44, 53
ZULULAND, 36, 44, 45
Zumbo, 19, 24, 27, 39
ZWANGENDABA, 36, 37